JUST GET ON WITH IT!

A CARING, COMPASSIONATE KICK UP THE ASS!

ALI CAMPBELL

HAY
HOUSE

HAY HOUSE

Carlsbad, California • New York City • London • Sydney
Johannesburg • Vancouver • Hong Kong • New Delhi

First published and distributed in the United Kingdom by:
Hay House UK Ltd, Astley House, 33 Notting Hill Gate, London W11 3JQ
Tel: +44 (0)20 3675 2450; Fax: +44 (0)20 3675 2451; www.hayhouse.co.uk

Published and distributed in the United States of America by:
Hay House Inc., PO Box 5100, Carlsbad, CA 92018-5100
Tel: (1) 760 431 7695 or (800) 654 5126
Fax: (1) 760 431 6948 or (800) 650 5115; www.hayhouse.com

Published and distributed in Australia by:
Hay House Australia Ltd, 18/36 Ralph St, Alexandria NSW 2015
Tel: (61) 2 9669 4299; Fax: (61) 2 9669 4144; www.hayhouse.com.au

Published and distributed in the Republic of South Africa by:
Hay House SA (Pty) Ltd, PO Box 990, Witkoppen 2068
Tel/Fax: (27) 11 467 8904; www.hayhouse.co.za

Published and distributed in India by:
Hay House Publishers India, Muskaan Complex, Plot No.3, B-2, Vasant Kunj, New Delhi 110 070
Tel: (91) 11 4176 1620; Fax: (91) 11 4176 1630; www.hayhouse.co.in

Distributed in Canada by:
Raincoast Books, 2440 Viking Way, Richmond, B.C. V6V 1N2
Tel: (1) 604 448 7100; Fax: (1) 604 270 7161; www.raincoast.com

A catalogue record for this book is available from the British Library.

ISBN 978-1-78180-495-7

Dedicated to the greatest coaches I've ever known... my Mum and Dad... thank you!

And to Claire...
all my love forever and for keeps.

Listen to your wisdom,
in your heart, your soul,

Listen to your knowing –
it's yours, you know,

Listen to others,
but then do what you want,

Listen, then just get on with it,
it's as simple as that…

CONTENTS

ACKNOWLEDGEMENTS

To all the people who have guided, nagged, praised, pushed, pulled, kicked, teased, enlightened and nurtured me into the person I am today, thank you! You are too many to name, but I hope you all know who you are and how much I appreciate the influence you have had on my life, even though I might not have known or appreciated it at the time.

I would, however, like to say a very personal thank you to some very special people:

Tony, Linda and Alan for welcoming me into your family and sharing some very special times.

Syd Banks, a fellow native Scot who through his philosophy has touched my life more than any other. It's a shame we never got to meet.

Bob Inglis for the immortal phrase: 'Just get on with it' and your very special brand of encouragement all those years ago…

Tim, Coobie and Tash for all your friendship and support.

Michael Neill for being my mentor, coach and provider of opportunity, and for believing in me even when I didn't. I can never tell you how much I appreciate your love.

A big and special thank you to Michelle Pilley and everyone at Hay House for letting my voice loose on the world.

Attiq Rahman for all your support right from, well, right from even before the start.

Tom Ranachan for being my friend and channel for my guidance; you've given me something very special, my friend.

To my 'brothers' Iain and Ally Ross, for still being there after all these years, 28 and counting…

And a big thank you to all my clients, past and present, for your inspiration and for giving me the honour of trusting me with your head.

INTRODUCTION

This revised version is still not a book where I get to know best – this is a collection of lessons and learnings gathered together from clients, books, teachers, trainers and therapists, and of course from my own journey trying to stay 'positive' growing up in one of the most cynical (yet wonderfully caring) places on earth.

This is still not a fluffy or typically touchy-feely type of coaching book either; this is a caring, compassionate kick up the ass. If I could build up a successful life-coaching practice in Glasgow, then I reckon the simple truth of these lessons mean I could do it anywhere! This book is the product of that journey, filled with the lessons I've learned from having to deliver big results with few resources. My clients don't want or need fluff; they want real change in their lives – and that's what I try my best to give them.

That's what you have here: the best bits, the distilled (well, I had to get a whisky reference in somewhere!) learning and techniques that really work. However, that in itself would be a little dull, so I put it all in context for you, with stories and tales from the front line of personal development. I think I've seen it all, from the rock star pulling up at my front door for his session in his tour bus to a client being hand-cuffed and arrested right in the middle of a session… perhaps they'd left it a little too late for 'therapy'; certainly they made me realize

I was used to 'tough' when I regarded coaching politicians in the Middle East as 'getting away from it all'!

I'm sure you won't mind if I've changed a few of the details to protect the... well, to protect me. If I hadn't, there almost certainly wouldn't have been any more books following this one.

So how is it that I came to be doing what I'm doing, and how is it that I came to be doing it the way I do it? Well, to understand that you have to understand where my whole idea of what a 'coach' is came from.

WHAT IS A COACH?

To some people the word 'coach' means something like therapist, expert, mentor or supporter. To me it instinctively means the grumpy, hard taskmaster with the whistle who helped me achieve my own early goals. While caffeine usually ensures that I'm not too grumpy, and I'm certainly not 'hard', I am the no-nonsense guy who asks the simple questions that may prove hard to answer – but once you do answer them, you can go beyond what's stopping you and start to really live to your full potential, your own personal best.

The title of this book was inspired by my athletics coach. You may have guessed he's also the guy who set my meaning of the word 'coach'. Although he hasn't coached me for nearly 20 years, his words 'just get on with it' still ring loud in my head. Probably because they were shouted at me so regularly.

This was the man who, apart from my own parents, was one of the greatest influences on my early life. He was a caring and totally committed man, loving in a very 'Scottish' way. He and his athletes had enjoyed great success on the track. Olympic and European medals hung proudly in many living rooms because of his commitment and dedication to the band of young men and women who followed his every word... well, most of the time.

Bob's success was built on a combination of applied knowledge and hard work. It was teamwork: he applied the knowledge and we supplied the hard work.

This was the time when drugs in sport were just becoming part of the public's consciousness, mainly due to Ben Johnson's humiliation in the 1988 Olympics. Ours was a completely clean training group – well, as clean as you can be when you're up to yours knees in mud from running through fields while bleeding, sweating and throwing up all at the same time... some of my happiest memories were spent like this. I know it sounds bloody awful, but we were achieving something, we were making our dreams come true... one gruelling training session at a time.

Our training was tough and my protests (which were frequent) were almost always met with 'just get on with it.' And that's what I've been doing ever since, applying knowledge and hard work and just getting on with it. Now, with these lessons, you can, too.

I promise I'll keep the throwing up and bleeding to a minimum, but we are going to get down and dirty as we explore the lessons that can be the short-cut to finding your success. This book is designed to give you exactly what it says: a caring, compassionate kick up the ass! Ready? Good! Let's get on with it!

CHAPTER 1

THE LIVING, THE DEAD AND THE SMALL VOICE WITHIN

Like any ability or muscle, hearing your inner wisdom is strengthened by doing it.

ROBBIE GASS

OK, for the uninitiated this is what can best be described as a 'self-help' book... But it's a self-help book in more ways than just where you'd find it in a bookstore. This is a book about *you* helping your*self* live the life that you've always dreamed of.

Before I go any further, I'd like to make a bold (and probably commercially quite fool-hardy) statement: my hope for you is that this is the last self-help book you'll ever need!

Now, before you go off on a train of thought about the size of my ego and the claim I've apparently just made – that I've written the best, and therefore the last, self-help book you'll ever need – I haven't. What I have actually said is quite the opposite.

My goal for this book is that you come to realize that the answers you seek are not found in the pages of *any* book. The answers are *inside* you, and once you find them there you will never have to seek answers from the outside ever again.

This is not a collection of 'how to' or 'the best way to' live your life pearls of wisdom. Think of each chapter more in terms of stepping stones or building blocks which have one purpose: to guide you to the realization that seeking answers from outside of you just masks the omnipotent guide already within you. All you need to do is take the time and allow yourself to listen to what you already know and what your inner wisdom is already trying to tell you.

Let me ask you a question: why did you pick up this book? I'll bet that at least at one level it was because you hoped it might have an answer for you… Or even that it might have THE answer for you and your particular problems. Well, the good news is that it doesn't!

It doesn't have THE answer, but it might just help you to find YOUR answer, for yourself. And the cool thing about finding it for yourself is that you get to keep it. It's not *my* answer, it's yours, and that means it fits you perfectly.

I have my own strategies and techniques and learnings, and it's my job to help you to find the source of yours for your own journey. You wouldn't ask to borrow my shoes and expect them to fit perfectly, would you? So why would you think that my answers, or anyone else's for that matter, would be exactly right for you?

The answer to that one is simple: we are conditioned to associate help and solutions with something *outside* of us, something that, if only we could find it, if only we had that special missing piece, would make everything else fall into place. So of course with this belief we set out to find the keepers of such secrets, such pearls of wisdom that will make everything OK.

Can you imagine my clients' initial disappointment when I tell them that I don't have the 'magic widget' they seek? Maybe you're feeling a little of this yourself? But while I haven't got the magic widget, I think I have got a sure-fire route to helping you find it... for yourself, in yourself.

I came to this realization in the most unlikely of circumstances... My friend Tom and I were sitting having coffee one day and generally putting the world to rights, when conversation turned to work and how we both effectively do the same thing: we help people find answers, and then comfort and happiness. The only difference is *how* we do it and what we call the 'source' of the answers our clients find.

As you know I am a life coach, so what I do is use my skill with the techniques, therapies, metaphors and coaching I know works to help people to find their own way. I do it in my own style. I'm by no means a purist, though; more a purveyor of what I know works.

Tom, on the other hand, is a psychic – and a very good one at that. He's no normal 'fluffy' psychic, though, not one of the ones you see randomly fishing for a bite in an audience primed to find meaning in whatever he is saying. You know the kind of thing: 'I'm getting the letter B, no, I'm hearing the name Bill... is anyone called Bill? Has anyone lost someone called Bill?... OK, does anyone know someone called Bill? Oh, wait... has anyone received a bill? Or not paid a bill or is expecting a bill?'

Tom's nothing like that, he's the real deal. But, like me, he doesn't take himself too seriously and enjoys poking fun at the surreal side of life – or, in his case, the after-life.

We enjoyed our coffee and traded funny stories of the weird and the wonderful, and even pondered the idea of putting on an event, a kind of 'Stand Up Therapy' show, when the title of this chapter popped into my head: 'The Living, the Dead and the Small Voice Within.' Then, right there in that little title, we both found some clarity of our own.

People come to me for answers, or to get a different perspective, to see things from the outside... and people go to see Tom for answers from 'the other side'. But what we both do – and rather brilliantly, if I may say so – is to help people find their own meaning, find their own guide on the inside. Tom might call it guiding them to connect with spirit, while I might call it coaching. But whatever you call it, the key to long-lasting change and living a happy and fulfilled life lies in following your own path and sticking with it even when what you think you 'should' be doing is trying to pull you out of shape and off track.

Easier said than done, you might think, but here in this book I'm going to help you to do just that in as many ways as I can find. Not so you finish this book and go away smarter or with a clever new technique; I'd love for you to finish this book and go away 'different', thinking differently and with the insight to hear and the confidence to follow your own inner wisdom… or, as Reinhold Niebuhr put it:

> *God grant me the serenity to accept the things I cannot change, the courage to change the things I can, and the wisdom to know the difference.*

And, I if may add my own coda:

> *Grant me the insight to know my own knowing;*
> *And then let it guide me down my own path so that I may enjoy my own true journey.*

Think of this chapter like the trailer of a movie: it helps you to know what's coming and gets you curious about what's next, but it's not the same as the full experience. The real answers you seek are not in me, in this book or in any of the numerous places people go to seek it.

THE ANSWER IS ALREADY IN YOU

Have you ever had a lightbulb moment, a sudden moment of clarity when everything made sense and you knew exactly what to do? So what happened? What was it that was different in that moment that allowed the clarity to come through? And why can't you do it at will? After all, if you can do or have something once, why can't you have it all the time?

Well, the answer could be as simple as 'because you don't let it.' Have you ever thought that you might be trying too hard?

How often do you find yourself in your head talking to yourself in a really negative way, even beating yourself up? 'What should I do? What's the right thing to do? Why am I so stupid I can't think of what to do? Argh!' The thoughts can be so loud they're deafening, and the more you seek answers the more confused you get, and the more urgent finding a solution feels. Sound familiar?

Sometimes we can't find the answers for looking for them. The problem here is simple: you're listening to the *wrong* voice.

Now, before you get worried, I don't think you're really hearing voices! We all talk to ourselves in our heads; the problem is that those thoughts can be so loud that you can't hear the voice of your inner knowing. Those moments of insight come when the conscious chattering thoughts are quiet for long enough to let the small voice within come through and be heard. But wouldn't it be nice not only to be able to call upon those moments of insight at will, but actually to have that inner voice as your natural setting? How cool would it be if you were always able to navigate by your own inner knowing, and enjoy the guidance of your own wisdom whether it consciously made sense at the time or not?

INSIGHT

How about making the exception the new rule and enjoying having insight whenever you need it? I like the word in-sight. 'In' and 'sight' – looking inward for the answer. It's amazing how accurate language can be when we really listen to it.

I'd like you to think for just a second. Think of a time when you knew exactly what was best for you and yet did something completely different. I'm sure you'll have a few examples. I'd like you to take just a second and think back to a time when you had the insight to see the right way but not the wisdom or courage to follow it. How did things turn out? Now, I'm going to go out on a bit of a limb here and say I'll bet not too well, eh?

We all have an inner knowing and we've all heard it from time to time, but what stops us from following it all the time?

Well, we are all taught and conditioned over time that we have to be able to explain our actions, to be able to make *logical* sense of things and justify them in terms of logic, reasoning and understanding. And all too often that's exactly what we do. We make choices in terms of what we think we 'should' do rather than what we know we 'want' to do or what we are guided to do.

I'd like it very much if you could, even just for the rest of this chapter, please just suspend your logical side and accept that sometimes we can't explain our knowing, and that in those moments we might just be making the wisest choices ever, even if we can't logically explain them to anyone else (or even to ourselves).

I know this might sound a bit 'fluffy', but believe me when I say that your inner wisdom is just as reliable, in fact more so, than any other measure you have – and I'm here to give you a kick up the ass to really listen to it for a change!

That's not to say that I am going to encourage you to listen to *all* the thoughts in your head – quite the opposite: I am going to encourage you to listen to your wisdom but not necessarily your internal dialogue. Over time you will get to know the difference between the voice of knowing and the voice of the 'know-it-all' storyteller in your head. Stories are powerful, and since time began great storytellers have wielded great power with their ability to engage with their audience and change emotions. In ancient times the storytellers would tell tales and invent theories in order to give meaning to the events of the day: 'This happened because it was the will of the gods' or 'That happened because you didn't do the right thing.' Stories stretch back almost as far as humanity itself, ever since people began to communicate with words we have been taking events and giving them meaning by, well, by making it up. Homer's great epics were first written down around 700BC. They became the textbooks in the schools of Greece and the cornerstone of Western literature as we know it. Whole civilizations have been built and shaped by the stories that were told and the beliefs that were formed as a result.

It's exactly the same with the storyteller in your head. The problem with our internal storyteller is that not only does it tend to be there all the time, it tends to be very compelling *and* to think it's right… This in itself is not a problem; the problem is that we believe it.

Think of your inner knowing as the quiet but powerfully wise (if not always obvious) part of you, the voice of your true knowing. The problem is that it's struggling to be heard above the incessant chatter of the loud and rather pushy storyteller. Sure, you might catch little moments of it when the storyteller pauses for breath, but if you're seeking that sort of clarity for good, then that's where I come in and it's exactly what I hope you'll get from this book.

WHO DO YOU THINK YOU'RE TALKING TO?

You already know (even if you're not consciously aware of it yet) that the words you use to describe your world have a massive effect on your experience of it. The words you use and the way you use them on the inside shapes your experience on the outside. We all think in words, and we all talk to ourselves in our heads.

The full impact of words was really brought home to me during a conversation I had a couple of years ago. I was in Abu Dhabi, and had been invited to dinner with some eminent literary people – not at all my natural habitat. As I sat listening to conversations about books I'd never heard of, let alone had an opinion on which language they translated into best, trying to look as intelligent as I could between yawns (it was the jetlag, honest!), my brain went whirring off to try to find some common ground so that I could actually contribute to the conversation.

I joined up parts of the conversation and got to thinking, if a book is translated into another language, how can someone have a preference for one over the other? Surely you would just prefer the one written in your native tongue, because you would understand that one best, right?

When I put that to the group, they all (and at great length) explained that indeed this was *not* the case. Some languages are far more descriptive than others, they said, so when a book is translated from an expressive language such as English or French into a less 'flexible' or expressive language such as Arabic, some of the subtleties will be lost. Certain languages just don't have the scope and breadth of expression necessary to convey the full scope of experience, they said. The opposite is also true: some translations add more description and enrich the original text with greater depth of emotion and feeling, albeit usually influenced a little by the personal linguistic preference of the translator.

I had taken for granted how deep and descriptive the English language really is. It's the only language I speak fluently (although some would doubtless disagree!). Just as the Inuit people have many different words for snow, in Scotland we have just as many, if not more, for rain.

So, if the flexibility and scope of a language affects the emotional experience of reading books written in it, is this also true of the people who speak a language and their experience of the world around them? When we read a book, we sound the words out in our heads, just as we do with our thoughts, so you could say that reading is a guided thought process.

I hope you're beginning to see my point, because you already know that a book, especially fiction, can be very powerful. The words we read and sound out in our internal dialogue create pictures and then powerful feelings within us, in ways far more powerful than we experience even at the cinema. How many times have you gone to see a movie and been disappointed because it wasn't as good as the book? That's because when you read your internal thoughts and experience create your own reality – and you know it can feel very, very powerful and 'real'.

This is why I'm urging you to stop engaging with the stories you are making up about your life. I know they can feel very 'real', but I assure you the only power they have, is the power you have given them. Every time you engage with a thought, a story you've made up something that's not real – in fact, what could be called a figment of your imagination – can become very real when you treat it as being so. It's not. It's just a thought until you make it otherwise.

Back to my group of scholars, I asked them a very simple question: does the scope of a language affect the behaviour and actions of the people who speak it? It seemed an obvious question to me, but apparently not so to my learned friends. As a coach I'm used to asking questions that have not been asked before, in order to get answers that my clients might never have explored before – and it appeared that on this evening I had managed just that.

The scholars allowed themselves to think, really think, not refer to some other source or textbook, or quote someone so obscure that no one dared show their ignorance by asking who on earth that person was (can you tell how out of place I felt?). As they thought – and remember these were some of the finest academic and literary brains in the world – one by one they concluded that the daft Scotsman might actually have a point. If the language we use affects our experience of a book, then surely it also affects our experience of the world around us.

If we have only extreme words to describe things, then we have scope for only extreme ways to feel about them.

Put simply, if we have only 'good' or 'bad', then we can have only good or bad feelings… Does that make sense? If we have only 'anger' or 'peace', we can feel only either angry or peaceful. Of course we have far more scope in our vocabulary than that but you must realize that the words we choose and the way we talk to ourselves massively affects the way we feel and the way we experience the world around us and therefore the assumptions we make and the conclusions we form about both.

A CARING KICK – IN THE RIGHT DIRECTION

Turn your awareness inwards and (even just for the next few minutes, or even better an hour if you can manage it) and just notice how you speak to yourself in your head. Think about some of the words you use in your internal dialogue, and try to pay particular attention to the words that come up again and again. We all have them – and normally they're just not very helpful.

Now I want you to imagine that everyone around you can hear your thinking. Imagine that everyone can hear your every thought… How different would you be if that were really true and you were that conscious of the effect your thoughts could have? Stop and imagine what that might be like. How much trouble would you get yourself into? How differently would people view you?

Most of us would be horrified and want to die of embarrassment if others could actually hear our thoughts. But why are we often so different on the inside than the person we pretend to be on the outside? Are you tired of the inner conflict? Tired of acting and reacting in ways that you don't want and probably don't even understand? Let me show you the inevitable sequence of events, and how a little thought, which may *appear* real, once engaged with can shape your life and become *very* real.

- **Thoughts, when engaged with, create feelings**
- **Feelings lead to actions**
- **Actions shape our lives and are what we are judged by**

One way or another, those thoughts you are trying so hard to hide will find their way out into the world, and have an effect. People might as well be able to hear your thoughts, because your actions are going to reveal them soon enough anyway.

However, you should also realize that... *Just because you thought it, doesn't make it true.*

We all make the mistake of blindly believing our thoughts, but it's definitely not smart. And it looks even less smart when you realize that the only person attributing pleasure or pain to a thing is YOU. It's only the stories you are telling yourself that keep you where you are, and it's only the stories you've told yourself that have got you there in the first place.

You know the kind of thing: 'This job stresses me out and I'm really not enjoying it. But it's a good job, one I'd always wanted and I've done well to get here.' Have you really done well if you find yourself in a stressful job? Hmmm, perhaps you should be more careful who you listen to.

THE PATH THAT'S RIGHT FOR YOU

Can you see now that the stories you tell yourself and the things you make up about them are maybe not the best way to navigate your way through life? I'm going to try to help you to come back to the path that's right for you.

Now, I'm not saying you have to give up on the things on the outside. It's just that when you're OK on the inside, then you can be OK in yourself *and* have all those external things around you. But you're not OK *because* of those things.

It's amazing what people will do in the pursuit of pleasure or the avoidance of pain, even when they know they're the one doling out both. Who beats you up if you miss your favourite soap because the traffic was bad? Who makes themselves angry if they miss their golf game because of a deadline? Who says that you must stay in a relationship cause you're nothing without the other person? Who decides that the source of your well-being is outside of you? You do! And you can change that right now… *and* it can be simpler than you could ever imagine.

Let me ask you a question. Which seems easier to have control over: the traffic, the deadline, the actions of your partner *or* the thoughts about those things in your head? Now, unless you're the control freak dominatrix boss of the town planning department (in which case this book is a very odd choice of reading material), then I'm guessing you opted for your thoughts?

Cool – Remember what I said earlier: stop making it up, stop telling yourself stories and believing them to be true.

I know this might be a big step for you, so, as a stepping-stone to setting yourself free, first notice this: if you are going to engage with the random thoughts in your head, at least pay attention to the stories you're telling yourself and the way you tell them. They are just stories. Unfortunately you are in the habit of believing them. Be aware that your thoughts and the meanings you give them *could* be true but are not *definitely* true.

In this book I'm going to guide you away from those old habits and help you to live from a clean and relaxed space where you do not have to actively do anything in order to be OK, you do not have to suppress your thoughts or wage an internal battle every day. If you're striving to be OK, you're going about it in entirely the wrong way. There simply won't be a battle to win and every day can be easy, even the ones when effort is required. In fact the 'effort' days can be the most 'effortless' of all...

EFFORTLESS EFFORT...

Effortless effort is the state where nothing is too much trouble. I'm sure you can think of many times when you've actually been doing exactly what you want to do and, even though the effort has been huge, it has felt, well, effortless.

By contrast I know that some days I find that just emptying the dishwasher is too much effort, let alone actually washing the dishes. But on other days I'd happily travel halfway round the world if it's for something I really want to do.

Come to think of it, if I really, really want to do something, nothing is too much 'effort'. The magical part here is that when you are following the path of 'want' rather than 'should', nothing is ever too much trouble and everything just feels much easier.

When your motivation comes from the inside instead of the outside, you are propelled towards your goal with seemingly effortless ease. This is something I'm going to keep bringing you back to again and again, because the path that's right for you will be the one where you are in flow, where you can relax and enjoy steering your own course, rather than feeling like you're paddling upstream and getting nowhere fast.

Do you remember a time when nothing was too much trouble? Maybe it was in the first flush of a wonderful romance, going the extra mile to get the job of your dreams or studying to pass that exam. I'm sure you can think of a time in your own life. Think back to that time now. Are you surprised at the lengths you went to? But didn't it feel like no effort at all?

How cool would it be to live from that place all the time?

It's really easy – in fact it can feel as if something far bigger than you is propelling you forward. What's not so easy at first (at least it wasn't for me) is keeping yourself in the right frame of mind, where effortless effort happens naturally every day. The good news is you can benefit from my doing the groundwork for you: I've learned lots of tricks and tips which I'll share with you.

This book is about helping you make the changes on the inside so that you stop working so hard and just enjoy steering yourself on your journey. Keeping on track might not always be easy, but the more you do it the easier it becomes.

Soon it'll be second nature.

First, though, we need to get you on the right journey in the first place. In order to start, we need to find out where you are now. Are you currently on an uphill struggle or an easy ride?

AN EMOTIONAL HEALTH AUDIT

What I'd like you to do is plot the energy you're using (that you are giving out or that's being drained from you) against the recharging energy of effortless effort (things that nurture you every day).

This is how my past five days work out: for example, today I've worked on this revised version of the book, I've coached some clients and I've done some trading on the Dow. I've also booked some places on an upcoming course and taken the cover off my car, which I've been meaning to do for ages. So I'll give myself a 7 for 'energy out'.

On the other hand I've gone for a drive – which is always fun – in the countryside, I've made healthy, nutritious food, been to the gym and had some time just hanging out with Claire at home, so I'll give myself a -8 for 'energy in'. All in all, a well-balanced day.

	Today −4	Today −3	Today −2	Yesterday	Today	Total
Energy out	5	6	6	9	7	34
Energy in	−6	−8	−9	−7	−8	−38
Total	−1	−2 (−3)	−3 (−6)	+2 (−4)	−1	−4

Figures in (brackets) are the cumulative total. You only really need the final total, but plotting each day will help to show you the flow of up and downs as well as the overall trend. The bigger the negative number the better, remember the path to your success is an easy downhill ride… the steeper the downward gradient, the easier your path through life will be.

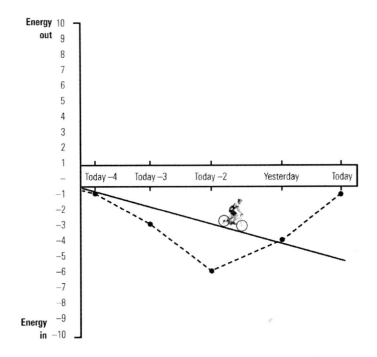

Now it's your turn: have a think back over the last five days. An 8 out of 10 in the 'energy out' row would be a tough day, but if it's balanced by −9 for energy in, then you are on the right track.

HOW STEEP IS YOUR LIFE?

Please come back and revisit this as often as you like, to check in with how you are doing. What I have found is that it doesn't matter how big the numbers are in the 'energy out' so long as they are balanced by the 'energy in' numbers; that's the key.

The path that's the right one for you will be the one where you can effortlessly enjoy the journey, going as hard and fast as you like but with energy expenditure being effortlessly balanced by what's nurturing you. That's what it's all about and if you're up for the challenge it will be my honour to guide you for as long as you need me.

YOUR SUCCESS IS ALREADY WITHIN YOU

Let me end this chapter with this thought – Your success is already within you. Your job over the course of this book is to use what you already know and already have, then get it out into the world to make the difference you want.

Following your path is simple – but not necessarily easy. That's what I'm here for.

Fears will come up for you; you may have to challenge some beliefs you have held for very long time – but when you do and come out the other side with a new way of being, the world you emerge into will be a very different place.

The rest of this book is not just about learning and getting smarter, it's about changing and being different. You can enjoy a new way of being in the world, and the really cool part is that once the ideas here have become obvious for you, they can never be hidden again. It's a bit like those pictures you may remember from school, if you look at it one way you see an old lady, but then when you adjust your perspective even just a little bit, you see a young woman instead. Once you have seen the new way, you can never un-see it again.

You can begin to look forward to looking at the world very differently… are you ready? Good, let's get on with it!

Oh – but before we do, just keep in mind the following as you enjoy soaking up the rest: it will all become clear as you read on, but let's get a bit clever here and set the scene and allow you to know what you're going to be absorbing in the chapters to follow… please read through the list below two or three times just now. Don't worry, I will explain everything and guide you through it, but for now I just want you to allow part of your brain to get an insight into where you're heading as you read.

GETTING THE MOST FROM THIS BOOK

1   Frame in the positive.
2   Listen to your instincts and keep checking in with them.
3   Challenge what you think you know.
4   Don't just believe your thoughts.

5   Take action.
6   Make more of a difference.
7   Stay emotionally positive.
8   Make your effort effortless.
9   Get curious: what might you be missing because you're focused on something that you think is more important?
10 Make being the authentic you your daily goal.

CHAPTER 2

WHAT DO YOU WANT TO BE WHEN YOU GROW UP?

Always be a first-rate version of yourself, instead of a second-rate version of somebody else

JUDY GARLAND

WHO ARE YOU REALLY?

OK now, before – in answer to this question – you go off into the realms of metaphysics, the spiritual, the land of Oz or the downright weird, I don't mean 'who are you really?' in the sense of 'who can any of us say we are?' I mean, how do you describe yourself? What's your 'party answer'?

It always makes me smile when people at a party ask the same two questions and yet expect to really learn something insightful: 'What's your name?' and then 'What do you do?' As if either is really going to tell them much about the person they've just met. Sure, it might be nicer to know the name of the person you're speaking to, but I suspect that, most of the time, the goal of the second question (whether they realize it or not) is to find out which box to pop the other person into.

Let me show you what's wrong with this straight away. Quite apart from the fact that what I do is not who I am, even with the best of intentions I'm going to have to delete many things and change others in order to keep my answer brief. Meanwhile, the person asking the question will be making some big generalizations and assumptions about both what I do and what that says about me as a person. What results is almost always wrong – or, at very best, an incomplete and therefore very distorted picture.

Can you imagine the look on peoples face when I say 'I'm a hypnotist'? Usually I do it just for fun, but it really *is* fun when they can't pop me into a neatly restrictive box.

This all gets a little more serious when we do that same misleading thing to ourselves, when the way we define ourselves actually becomes who we think we are, and then becomes the very source of our emotional health. You know the kind of thing: 'My name's Dave and I'm 34 and a business executive,' 'My name's Sarah and I'm a bank manager.'

If the part that makes you happy is found in the 'business executive' part or the 'bank manager' part, or any other definition on the outside of you, then you have got it the wrong way round.

Who could you be if you didn't define yourself in those terms? Who would you be if you wore a new badge? Or even better, no badge at all? Who would you be if you could live on different terms?

WHO ARE YOU ON THE INSIDE?

There has been a huge shift in the world in recent years, not just in the sense of the economy but, as I see it, more in where people go in search of answers and what they are looking for in life. I was watching the Formula 1 Grand Prix a few weeks ago, Monaco I think it was – somewhere that could not possibly be more materialistic and superficial if it tried. Amidst the super yachts, super cars and super-size egos sat Lewis Hamilton. As he sat being interviewed in the Riviera sunshine, suitably adorned with various sponsors badges and bling, he was asked what his goals were.

'I'm just trying to make my life as simple as possible' he said, 'I'm cutting out anything that pulls me out of shape and focusing on being happy.'

Even Russell Brand, once the hell-raising womanizer of old London town, now regularly talks about spirituality, energy and his belief in an 'infinite creative force'. Who'd have thought it?

The world is changing and so are you. Now more than ever it's important to understand what you check in with to let yourself know that you're ok, and to be very aware of the relationship you have with your own thinking.

We are all in the habit (consciously or not) of 'checking in' with something outside of ourselves just to make sure we're OK. Whether you consciously do it or not I'll bet you do. It might be your job that let's you feel 'secure', or your children who make your life 'worthwhile' or even your bank balance that tells you that you're 'successful' or even 'worthy' – but I want you to know right now that you can be OK without those things. Of course you can still have and want them, but as I said earlier, you can be OK *and* have those things, not *because* of those things.

The first thing we need to do is find the real part inside of you, the part that let's you know you're OK and that is yours to keep, no matter what's going on around you.

You can't get fired from the role of 'compassionate carer'; you can't get laid off from the role of 'creator' or get swept aside from 'abundant creative thinker' or 'happy and decent person' by the broom of another corporate downsizing.

The world is changing fast and one thing is clear: the source of your happiness and success will be found in who you are, and not what you do.

How many bankers and other 'professionals' are now unemployed? How many 'good' graduates from 'good' schools who were good at playing by one set of rules are now learning that the game is changing fast and that they are not as commercially desirable as they once were? It doesn't really matter if you know all about 'Hedging and

Forward Contracts' (no, apparently it has nothing to do with the garden) if your company is bust and the government is paying your rent. But what will make all the difference, both in terms of your employment prospects and your sanity, is who you are.

FINDING THE TRUE YOU

So, who are you? I don't expect you to be able to come up with the perfect definition straight away. How you define yourself sets the course by which you live your life, so it's very important to make sure you know where you are starting from – and then, obviously, where you are going.

Finding and reconnecting with the true you, your true starting point and your true values, is like re-laying the foundations of your future. Once you have that bit right, building your dreams will be easy, and they'll have a better chance of standing up for a while no matter what life throws at you.

It's difficult to navigate anywhere without true bearings of where you're really starting from and where you're really going. Even the best maps are only useful if you know both of those things. For now, though, let's stick to getting clear on who you are and what it is that you 'check in' with for your well-being.

I have a client who is a multi-millionaire, very successful in almost every area of his life, and yet although I have known him for years I have no idea who he would be if he weren't a multi-millionaire.

I don't mean if someone took away all his money, I mean if they took away his 'title' of multi-millionaire. His entire sense of self-worth is attached to his bank balance; when it's on the way up he's happy and outgoing, but when it's on the way down he's worried and anxious.

Nothing unusual in that, you might think, if we do well and get a bonus or have good month most of us might feel a little more 'extravagant' – but when I tell you that if my client never worked another day in his life he could still live very comfortably, it makes the scenario a little different. Nothing would physically change in his world if he never earned another penny, yet he wakes up in the morning feeling poor and 'needing' to go to work… not for the money but for the daily fix of self-worth.

I know lots of people like this; in fact everyone I've ever met has a personal something that they check in with, which helps them feel they're all right. For most people it's something outside of them, but for the happy, contented *and* successful ones it's on the inside. That's what I want for you.

For my client it's his bank balance; for others it might be their fitness or the kids' grades or their annual review or any of an infinite number of things that mean something to them. For you it might be your share portfolio or the value of your house – in which case I'm guessing you're not feeling too happy right now?

You see, while we all do this to a greater or lesser extent, it really is not healthy to place the source of our self-worth outside of us. What happens if the thing on the outside changes? Or even disappears entirely? If your self-worth is attached to your job or your money, what happens if you lose them? And, nowadays especially, that can happen through no fault of your own...

CHECKING IN WITH YOUR SELF-WORTH

So what is it that *you* check in with, outside of you, to know you're OK? Just think about it for a moment...

Now ask yourself: how would I feel if I didn't have that? If your answer is anything other than a resounding 'I'd be fine,' then you really do need to keep reading.

Your well-being has nothing to do with what's happening outside of you. You can lose your job *and* still be OK. Sure, the financial issues that come with that will be very present, but you can be OK while you deal with them. The world can be going to pot *and* you can still be OK.

Of course, while finding this kind of contentment can happen very easily when you place the source of your self-worth on the inside of you instead of seeking it in the stuff on the outside, it won't happen by itself. There's stuff for you to do. You need to put in the effort and turn up for it, and obviously I'm going to encourage you to get on with doing exactly what needs to be done, but it won't be the difficult stuff on the outside you'll be working with; it will be stuff you have absolute control over: what goes on right there inside you.

Being stressed is not going to help you in any way at all. In fact, the worse things are on the outside the more you need to focus on what's happening on the inside. Once you break that link between stuff happening on the outside and your feelings on the inside, you really can be OK regardless of what's going on around you. Wouldn't that be cool? Thought so...

OK, so now that you get the idea, the first thing to realize is that security, financial or otherwise, comes not from containment but from *creation*. Security is not a big pile of money locked away in a dark room. Real security comes from your ability to create whatever you want or need, whenever you want or need it.

Let me put it like this: if the job you have is the only way you can feed yourself and your family, then I totally understand being stressed at the thought of losing it.

But it's not.

If it really came down to it now, what else could you do to generate an income? I'm just trying to wake you up a bit, so just for now put pride and the notion of what someone like you 'should' do to one side and have a good think about what you 'could' do to keep a roof over your head. When you have three ways (keep them legal, please), jot them down...

1...

2...

3...

How hard was that? Now, I know these might not be ideal jobs, and almost certainly not your true calling – but they should have helped you to realize that, if you really had to do one of them to earn a living, you could. And as soon as you realize that you have choices, then you have set yourself free from feeling total dependent and afraid.

CREATING WHAT YOU WANT

You have the ability to create anything you want, be it wealth, love, fitness, better grades and, of course, happiness. This book could have been titled 'Getting What You Want with a Smile', because it really is quite simple to get whatever it is that you want to create in your life.

Before you go flicking ahead looking for the lottery numbers (they must be here somewhere), 'quite simple' still involves doing stuff – just not the stuff you have been doing up until now. So please, right now, acknowledge the fact that to make your life better you are going to have to do some things – in fact, you are probably going to have to do lots of things – differently. They will be little things, very simple things, not necessarily easy but almost certainly different, and you'll have to keep doing them for a while until you notice the difference. Eventually doing things differently will become a habit and you won't even notice anymore. But at first it will feel a little unusual – why wouldn't it? You've never done things this way before.

Sorry if this is shattering your illusions, but there is no such thing as a self-installing 'success pump'... I have met many people who say they want to change everything and yet they are prepared to do nothing. That attitude just doesn't work. This book will not change your life just by you owning it. It has a better chance if you read it, but it *will* definitely change your life if you follow the few simple suggestions it contains. That said, of course we are going to do things the easiest way possible...

The easiest way is an inside-out approach. I'm going to help you to change things on the inside so that the outside world changes, too. What do you think is easier to change, the rest of the world or your thoughts about it? Well I'm hoping you said your thoughts, and you know what? Once you've done that you *can* change the world, or at least the bits of the world that bump against you...

But let's get back to the idea that freedom comes from your ability to create. By creation I don't mean giving up the day job to go off and make candles. There's certainly nothing wrong with that, it's just not the point here.

By creating I mean the power to change and shape things to be as you want them to be. Even if you have been stuck in the same job or situation for years, you have the ability to create change in that environment right now.

They say a change is as good as a rest. There is no doubt that keeping things fresh while keeping yourself in the space where you are actively exercising as much choice as you can have in your life is the key to being happy. And when you're happy you're more creative, and when you're creative you have choice – and when you have choice you are free.

But take note of this warning: if you don't keep things fresh, they might even kill you.

Being on the right path, going in your own flow, moving with the momentum and direction of your life is in fact the only way to live a happy, fulfilled, effortless and therefore successful life. They say a change is as good as a rest, but a change for the better, a change to stop fighting or swimming upstream is a change that can only ever be made on the inside. There is no amount of rearranging the furniture on the outside that is anywhere near as powerful as the insight to let go on the inside.

You see, as soon as you do that, as soon as you let go of being 'right' and instead look for the path of least resistance, you automatically start to make changes in the outside world, too. We are designed to grow and develop to keep things fresh, to encounter new challenges, new opportunities and new inspirations. That's our way of spiritually and energetically coming in for a pit stop and refuelling. It's not a luxury or even an option, we need it. You need it...

SAME CRAP, DIFFERENT DAY?

The problem with doing the same thing day in day out is that you begin to get complacent and fatigued – and if you get stuck in a rut, that's where you'll end up. A rut is really a grave with the ends knocked out…

A few years ago I was filming a TV pilot for a phobia-cure show and got chatting to the animal handler. He had grown up in a circus family and entertained us all day with stories of taming and training new animals. At one point he said, 'You wouldn't think it but apparently elephants are really easy to train, so long as you get them young enough.'

'How can that be?' I asked. 'How can such a huge animal, happy wandering for miles and knowing no boundaries, be so easy to train? I mean, how do you even keep them in the tent?'

'Well,' he said 'if you get them young enough you can chain them to a strong post so that the young elephant cannot move. Of course at first they try to get free, but very quickly they learn that they are helpless and stop even trying.'

I guess it's a bit like in prisons, too; it is incredibly unusual for someone even to try to escape after they have been in jail for a long period of time. Most escape attempts happen in the first 12 months of a sentence. Inmates learn helplessness in terms of escaping, and instead find ways to exercise control and choice in their confined environment.

It occurred to me then that this is exactly what we all do: we learn to think that we are helpless and so we stop trying and, just like the elephant, even though over time we grow in strength and experience both inside and out, we 'perceive' that our choices are limited, we 'perceive' that we are stuck, and so we don't even bother to challenge things anymore. We just accept that what we've learned was true once must still be true now…

I'll bet you're not really stuck. If only you gave the chain of life a really good tug, you might find that it's not as fixed as you think. Trust me when I say never just believe your thinking. Even if it was true once, it probably isn't now.

Anyway, back to the animal handler, by far the most interesting conversation we had that day was when I learned that this man who that day had nothing more than a couple of rats and a few spiders to deal with, was actually a lion tamer, just like his father had been before him.

I was fascinated. 'OK, so I get it with the elephant, but what's the secret to taming a lion? You don't just tie a lion to a pole and wait for it to give up, do you?' It turned out that the key to lion taming is 'changing your lion', and regularly. Apparently, to tame a lion you have to make yourself appear bigger and more boisterous than the lion. I don't suggest you try this, because, as he said, 'If the lion ever gets a measure of your inferior weight and strength, it will kill you.' So it's not so much a question of 'taming' a lion as delaying the inevitable.

The trick is to keep it fresh and change your lion before it finds you out. This guy knew what he was talking about – he had witnessed his own father being killed by the lion he was 'taming'. He said of his father, 'He just kept doing the same thing for too long.'

I wonder if that might be the case with most of us? Throughout the course of your journey with me here I will be gently nudging you – OK, kicking you in the right direction – to make you sit up and notice some of the simple things that can get you unstuck and make change very easy for you. Please do each one, even if it's only to play with it for a while. This is not a novel; the magic comes in the *doing*, not just in reading through to the end.

OK, here's the first of the caring kicks in the right direction: a change can be as good as a rest. Enjoy!

A CARING KICK – IN THE RIGHT DIRECTION

KEEPING IT FRESH

This involves deliberately using some of your time to do something totally new, or at least in a new way. It must be something that makes YOU feel alive. It's not what you think you 'should' do; it's something you really 'want' to do… Play time for you, if you like. It can still be work but it must feel different.

To make this work, you have to be honest with yourself and set aside a regular chunk of time, instead of pretending that five minutes snatched here or there will add up in the long run. They don't. You have the opportunity here to make *you* really important again. That's not being selfish, it's essential! You have the choice of whether you are important to you right now!

USING THE CHOICE YOU DIDN'T KNOW YOU HAD

Setting yourself free on the inside is the quickest way to setting yourself free on the outside. You have no idea how many people I meet who have taken themselves prisoner in their own heads. People for whom the only barrier between them and what part of them *really* wants (the life they've dreamed of) is the other part of them keeping them stuck – we'll call that part their jailer. The jailer is a great storyteller, too, and it's the part that generates all the negative and limiting thoughts, I'm sure you know the kind. We all do, but we don't all listen to them or believe them. Don't just believe those crappy thoughts in your head. You have the choice not to engage with them. Once you stop, you'll notice that the emotional walls that have kept you confined are not real, however real they might have appeared (and I know they can seem very real) they are just a product of what you think you can or cannot do, just a product of thought. And when you really let go of that, wow, will you notice the difference!

How much choice is the jailer in your own head taking away from you?

One of the quickest ways to depress anyone is to take away their perceived choice. I say 'perceived' because you always have more choice than you think you have. It's just that, like the elephant, you may have learned not to use it.

I'd love you to be more like the lion: you're going to get your own way, you just need to get a measure of how...

It's time to use that choice and break free from whatever's holding you stuck. All you have to do is give it a really good tug in the right direction and you might find it comes free much more easily than you might think.

Right now, make a quick list of the areas of your life that you'd like to give a tug on and see how easily they come free... Let's do three for now; they can be anything you want and obviously you can have as many as you need.

- **Area to be set free 1**
- **Area to be set free 2**
- **Area to be set free 3**

Now, just to get you going, I'm going to encourage you to trust your instincts and ask yourself 'What's the smallest thing I can do that will make a difference'?

There is a good chance that, somewhere inside, you already know what to do, it's just that inertia and perhaps a little bit of fear are preventing you from actually doing it.

I'm going to encourage you just to have a think about those three things now and then just get on with them. Don't think about them, don't make excuses or overanalyze them, just think about what to do and then do it. Are you up for it?

Good!

I'll be checking in with you later to see how you're going…

LESS IS MORE… (WELL, MORE OR LESS)

Now, if you're going to make a difference in your life, I just want to explain something else to you right up front.

When you think of making a difference in your life, do your top goals involve getting more of something? I'll bet they mainly do, but just on the off-chance that they don't, I would like to encourage you to frame whatever you want in the positive. Your brain will find it much easier to process it this way.

Having to work fewer hours, for example, could be framed as 'having more spare time'. Being less stressed could be framed as 'being more content'. Got the idea? Please get into the habit of framing things in the positive, stating what you *do* want instead of what you *don't* want.

OK, good, we're making progress, I know there's a lot to take in here, but that's OK. I will explain it all fully and you'll have lots of time to practise everything in the chapters to come. I just want to set things up for you here so that you can have some of the ideas in mind as you read on.

Let me just remind you that in order to make a difference in your life, and in the lives of others, you need to do *something* – but you do not need to *do more* in order to *have more*… In fact, the secret is that you might even need to do a lot less.

As I see it, there are only two ways to get a lot more out of life:

- **Option 1 - Do a lot more of the same**
- **Option 2 – Get a lot more for what you do**

The former was once my approach to almost everything. After all, that's the way I was brought up: if I wanted more, I had to work harder to get it. And if I wanted a lot more, I had to work a lot harder, while of course that makes sense, by its very definition it's hard work.

If your hourly rate is fixed, the only way to earn more is to do over time. Do more and get more makes sense, but it's really tough going – and more importantly there is a limit on how much more you can actually make. No matter how hard you work, there is a ceiling on your potential. Even if you could work 24 hours a day, 7 days a week, you'd still hit the buffer of your earning potential – and probably kill yourself in the process.

I think it was Winston Churchill who said something along the lines of '[A person] invariably does the right thing, after having exhausted every other alternative.' I was certainly very familiar with the hard work and exhaustion route. I was frustrated that the more I worked and the more tired I became, the less work I could actually do. My relationships were suffering and so my strategy for getting more was actually causing me to get less. I was definitely 'exhausted' and ready for an 'alternative'. It made sense in theory, but it just wasn't working.

'There must be another way,' I thought. And of course there is. The route to financial freedom – and freedom in all areas of your life – lies not in doing more but firmly in upping your market value, and specifically in making more of a difference.

This has always been the case. If we go back through history, the people who have consistently been rewarded best are the ones who make more of a difference in the world. I don't just mean financially. Do you think Mother Teresa felt rewarded, fulfilled and loved for the work she did? I'm sure she did. And did she make a big difference? Absolutely! Whatever it is that you want more of, the key is to make a difference, to be remarkable, to do something remarkable… Here I use the word literally: do something about which others will 'remark', get noticed and make the difference you want to make in the world, your own life will inevitably benefit with a beautiful and effortless synchronicity.

Just to reinforce the point, though, I want to be really clear: you can't make more of a difference by doing more of the same.

The word 'difference' is the clue. In order to make more of a difference, you have to be prepared to do things differently.

Making more of a difference is found in adding value to every situation, not just doing more of it. A different kind of effort is required. Quality rather than quantity, if you like, but it doesn't have to be hard work. In fact, when you've got it right and you're doing the right thing for you, the 'effort' can be truly effortless...

GETTING WHAT YOU WANT BY DOING WHAT YOU WANT

You still have to do things – this book has very little chance of having any effect on your life if you don't take action. This is a time to take action, but if you want to receive you must first be prepared – and happy – to give. I have always found that I have received more than I have given. That's not to say I don't give much, I give a great deal, but I always get more back.

This makes sense on a number of levels. Socially, people are always more likely to give if they have received first. Emotionally, you have the potential energy and the ability within you to take action whenever you want, so you have the choice, and energetically you have the capacity to use that choice to get things moving and flowing. The key to sustained giving – and therefore sustained receiving – is in the little word 'happy'. Effortless effort happens when nothing is too much trouble. But you must be prepared and happy to give, and disciplined enough to give only those things that you are happy to.

Of course, most people would like to think of themselves as 'givers', especially in this particular genre; but I also know that some people have an unhealthy expectation of what the world owes them. And I'm afraid some of the books out there recently haven't helped.

The problem, as I see it, with the simplistic idea of the so-called law of attraction, is that it leaves out the fundamental part about *taking action*. Now, I am as much of a fan of the alternative route as the next guy, but I have always found that the quickest and most reliable way to get something I want is to *do* something about it, not simply open up to the possibility of the universe delivering it on a plate.

OK, glad I got that off my chest. Now let me close this chapter by clarifying exactly how you can make sure your effort is, and remains, effortless.

One of the common mistakes I have made over the years is that I am not great at saying 'No.' This can become even more of a problem when you are following your path and doing what you want. I know at first that might seem a little counter-intuitive: why would you want to say 'No' to anything when you are doing what you want? Surely a resounding YES would be more appropriate?

Well, effortless effort – and therefore success – lies not in how many things you can start, but in how many things you can finish. The problem is that when I am in flow and following what I really want, the tendency is to add more and more and more cool stuff so that I am doing more and more. Even though it's more and more of what I *want* to be doing, it doesn't matter whether it's something you love or not; if you don't complete tasks you will find yourself carrying them around in your head and feeling stressed just the same.

The trick is not in 'What can I do that I love today?' but in 'What can I complete today?' It's not 'What can I start?' but 'What can I finish?' Now, I know that there are many things that simply cannot be completed in a single day, but there is nothing that cannot be broken down into a chunk that can. Even really big tasks or projects can be split into smaller 'complete-able' chunks… so what can you complete today?

It's amazing the effect this approach can have on your productivity and your stress levels. Keep your effort effortless by following your inner knowing and only taking on what you know you can complete… effortlessly.

What three things can you effortlessly complete today?

1...

2...

3...

Great, that's your 'to do' list, simple as that. Now, Just Get On With It!

CHAPTER 3

STOP MAKING IT UP

Why do you do many things you know inside that you shouldn't? Why do you stay in a relationship you know is not good for you? Why do you stay in a job you hate? Why is it that even though a situation is hurtful you stay put, right where you are?

Well, the answer (if not immediately obvious) is that at some level you probably associate that thing outside of you with being the source of your happiness, or even your self-worth…

Putting the source of your self-worth on the outside of you is one of the most common – and fastest – ways to hurt yourself. The things on the outside should only ever be physical reflections of your condition *inside*; otherwise, no matter what you have or what you get, it will still always feel out of place and out of shape. It's the resulting disharmony and inner conflict that causes the pain. Having a sports car can hurt more than not having it if you don't think you're worth it.

I'd like you to think about something. How many times do you find yourself saying some variation on 'They made me angry' or 'They really hurt me' or 'I wish they'd call and make the pain go away'? Whichever of these is relevant to you, the point I am making is that we associate things outside of us as the source of our pain.

It's the same thing with things we associate with pleasure. We think, 'If this happens, then I can be happy...'

As I've said before and will continue to remind you, *the source of both your pain and your comfort is actually on the inside, never the outside.*

I was working with a client recently who'd just broken up with her partner. In her words, he'd left her 'devastated'. All around, her friends were pitching in with really useful advice like, 'Why don't you just go and get drunk?', 'How about a takeaway and a bottle of wine?' or 'Right, I'm on my way and I'm bringing chocolate...'

Now, I should probably mention at this point that the client in question was initially seeing me for weight loss and was the lightest she'd been in 15 years, so I was doubly displeased by her friends' 'helpful' suggestions. What happened in our session was quite remarkable, and I share it with you to illustrate the links that people make, so that you can find your own meaning for you.

One of the first things that came up was that (even although she wasn't sure she wanted to be in the relationship in the first place, they'd been on and off for a while and we'd spoken about that only the week before) the *choice* had been taken away from her. That's what really hurt. It's a funny thing, but even when we don't want something we still want control over whether we have it or not, don't we?

This is actually one of the core principles I teach my clients about: choice. From now on I want you to let yourself be in a position to choose as often as you possibly can. You will be amazed at how something so simple can have a profound effect on your well-being. My client's pain wasn't coming from the fact that her relationship had ended; the pain was coming from the fact that it wasn't her choice (well, not that time, anyway).

Well, believe it or not you can always choose choice! Even if you cannot control the situation – in fact, especially when you can't – you can still choose how you feel in the situation depending on your relationship with your thoughts at the time.

The next thing that came up was in fact one of the reasons why she had struggled with her weight for so long. 'I'm almost the lightest I've ever been and still I can't find someone to love me, so that must mean I'm unlovable and worthless.'

Now, I don't know about you, but I know of no law of nature that draws a link between someone's self-worth and their waistline. It is this socially constructed and completely made-up link that causes lots of people lots of problems. In this case, the made-up assumption was that skinny MUST equal lovable and worthy, despite all evidence to the contrary. Especially as they'd got together when she'd been much, much heavier, and she had to admit there are lots and lots of skinny people who are single and unhappy… hmm …? So, that can't be true, then?

So her first real lesson had to be 'Stop just making it up.' You can do the same now. Next time you find yourself engaged in a train of thought and jumping to conclusions, stop and consider: although it might feel very real, are you in fact just making it up?

Next we came to 'I'm not happy, but I am thin and I did have a boyfriend. I thought that would make me happy, but it didn't… I had both of those things I wanted and was still unhappy. Now I don't and I'm miserable, too.' Can you see how happiness might not be about the things on the outside of you? This is the fundamental point of this whole book: it's a simple idea yet sometimes tricky one to grasp. Finding real happiness and well-being is an inside-out process, it's never really dependent on anything outside of you even though it can certainly feel like it, I'll show you how to reconnect with it as you read on. Suffice to say for now that true happiness is something you only ever find on the inside, not acquire on the outside, not ever.

Next up in our session we came to, 'I'm tired of fighting, maybe I should just give up and accept my lot in life' (there is often a misconception that change has to be hard; it *must* be, that's why you've not managed it yet). Of course that makes some sense, but what if it is easy and you've just not tried going about it the right way yet?

GETTING BACK TO THE REAL YOU

Change can be as easy as pressing the reset button, but 'resetting' all the way back to your natural state. Not just in terms of what you *think* you know: 'I just want to go back to what I know and have some chocolate cake and a bottle of wine and I know I'll feel better.' How many times have you done that? I don't mean specifically chocolate cake and wine, but how many times have you looked outside yourself for the solution to pain on the inside? A fair few times, I'd bet! And it kind of makes logical sense: we're conditioned from a very early age that comfort comes from the outside of us. If we hurt ourselves when we're little, a hug from mum or a sweetie or a biscuit makes it better. Then when we get older the sweetie or biscuit are replaced with a drink or a cigarette or sex or drugs or positive thinking books or any number of the things we adults turn to in our time of need…

My client continued, 'Actually, what I really want is to call him and for him to change his mind, because then all these thoughts about what it all means will go away and I can be happy again.' And in that throwaway remark she might just have found peace. Not in the bit about him changing his mind (they weren't happy before and I'm sure that even if he did change his mind, within a couple of weeks I'd be having another conversation about how she wanted to end it this time), but in the second half of the sentence. Without even realizing it or hearing what she was actually saying, she found her peace – or at least the start of her journey that would lead to her effortless and permanent peace of mind and happiness. 'These thoughts about what it all means will go away and I can be happy again.'

If I had a big tree root in my garden and I wanted to remove it to plant a flowerbed, I could quite reasonably expect it to be hard work. The tree is heavy, it's been there for a very long time and its roots run deeper than the foundations of my house. You might reasonably expect that I would need some tools and that I would need to struggle and 'put my back into it', and that if I did that consistently I would first of all see the root start to move a little, then I might be able to use that little movement to get some leverage. From there, I might be able to break the root loose from what had been keeping it stuck, and then with even more effort I might be able to lift it out and take it away. Sounds about right. Right?

Of course, this will take some time, but in our favour we do have nature on our side. Just like going to the gym – if I kept at it and kept at it, my body, without any additional mental input from me and without my asking, would just naturally get stronger to cope with the physical strain of the load I was putting it under, and help me to reach my goal. First of all, we recruit all the resources we have available in the form of additional muscle fibres and then, when we need even more, those muscle fibres start to grow thicker and stronger. That is how we build muscle.

However… when we want to make changes in our mind instead, those laws of physics and form simply do not apply and, in fact, the inverse is true. When we consistently apply an additional physical load to our body we get stronger, but when we consistently apply an additional mental load to our mind, we get weaker. Not because it's our fault, it's just how we're made, how we're naturally wired up. The body is designed to do more on the outside and less on the inside; we just don't tend to run it like that anymore… the laws of physics and form simply do not apply to the world of thoughts and mind; we just think they do, until we know better, that is.

BEING HAPPY… AGAIN

I always think that whenever we say 'I want to be happy' or 'I want to be relaxed' or 'I want to be content', we should always add 'again'.

We came into this world happy and contented, loving and joyful and, with the exception of the odd full nappy, we were quite happy. So what the hell happened to take us all from joyful innocence to where lots of us find ourselves now?

I know you're probably thinking some version of 'Life happens, stuff happens, even sh*t happens. Of course when I was a baby I was happy; I didn't need to deal with all the crap I do now and nothing had happened to scar me then… what planet's this guy on?' Or something like that, anyway. But what if it wasn't the stuff that scarred you and caused you pain? What if it was something as simple as the 'thoughts' about the stuff?

This idea is based on the contemporary philosophy of fellow Scot Sydney Banks, but its origins go back 2,500 years to Gautama Buddha. Of course, this is my take on how to free yourself quickly from the pain you often cause yourself.

Think about it this way. Some people are scared of heights and some people are not, so heights cannot be universally scary. Some people are scared of spiders and others are not, so spiders cannot be inherently scary either. So if it's not the heights or the spiders themselves that cause us pain, it must be our *thoughts* about them. Does that make sense? What if it wasn't breaking up with a partner that caused the pain? What if it was just the *thoughts* about it that caused the pain?

What if it wasn't chocolate cake and a bottle of wine that brought comfort, what if it was what they do to our thoughts that brings comfort? Then, if that is the case, doesn't that give us a clue that the source of both our happiness and unhappiness lies, not on the outside, but on the inside? It's right there inside you right now; whether you know it or not, it's there. How cool is that?

BREAKING THE HABIT

You can break the habit of making things up in your head, so that you can live in a place of choice, listen to your own inner wisdom and realize that the source of your happiness and well-being right there are inside you. How cool would it be to know that the world could be going to hell and you could still be OK? Well, life can be like this, because your well-being comes from within and it can exist totally independently of what's going on around you.

When you realize that things can be going against you and you can still be OK, that's when you'll know you have freedom of choice and freedom of emotion and, ultimately, freedom in every area of your life. When you start from a place of 'happy' and 'contented' and break the habit of reacting emotionally to the world around you, then you are free to be you, the real you, in any situation.

Life is not an either/or equation; your brain is far cleverer than that… and the answer doesn't lie in life coaches or psychics or chocolate cake or wine. It lies in you.

TIME TO LET GO AND GET BACK INTO SHAPE

Imagine a large spring – you know, the kind you used to play with as a child, I think it was called a 'Slinky'. In its natural state, it's relaxed and quite content to just happily sit, full of coiled energy but happy just to be still.

We're a lot like that, our natural state is full of energy, calm and relaxed. However, over time we tend to allow ourselves to get stretched out of shape, to get pulled in different directions. The more we get pulled out of shape, the more tension and stress we feel in our lives. All the time, all we want to do is return to our natural state of being relaxed, content, loving and just, well, happy. When a spring is stretched and under strain, the stress comes not from what's pulling at it but from its own force resisting the external one, trying to recoil back to normal. You don't have to push it back into shape, you don't have to force it or struggle to get it back to normal, it doesn't take years of therapy, it just has an innate memory of who it is and what it looks like and naturally wants to get back there, and fast! All you have to do is let go.

Now here's the key difference that will make all the difference. We already know that it's not the 'things' that are the issue. It's our thoughts about the things so if we play with this a little further we find that it's not the 'things' in your life that pull you out of shape it's the thoughts about those things that pull at your natural well-being and cause you to get stressed and out of shape. When you learn how to let go of those thoughts and break the habit of reacting to your thinking, then change is not just easy, it's inevitable, it's who you are.

YOU are the Slinky; YOU are that innately happy and healthy person, you have just got stretched out of shape. The stress in your life comes not from what's pulling you but from your innate desire to return to the way you're supposed to be. Stress doesn't come from what's pulling you but from the resistance of your innate well-being knowing it doesn't have to be like that, from your knowing that your current situation is not the best or right way for you – after all, if it were right you'd be happy, right?

This makes sense when you think about it, but I'll concede that for me it was a whole new way of looking at life. Starting from a place where everything is OK, you can just be the way you should be; it really can be as easy as that. If you don't believe me just yet, please bear with me…

RESTORING YOUR ORIGINAL SETTINGS

The way I've just described it is certainly *not* the way things have been for me in the past – and unless you grew up in a particularly enlightened place it's probably not been that way for you, either. So, how do you get from where you are now to the place where change is easy and you have complete choice and clarity? The initial step, believe it or not, is so simple you might struggle with it at first before it becomes really easy.

It's as simple as pressing the reset button and allowing things to go back to the way they should be and the way they once were, back to your natural settings. You know that 'restore factory setting' option on your mobile phone? Well, there's one for your head, too, restoring you back to the way you once were, whether you realize it or not.

The first thing to do is *become aware of your thoughts.*

That's right, just allow yourself to become aware of your thoughts, or even just that you *have* thoughts. I don't want you to do anything with them, just become aware of your thoughts and begin to recognize them for what they are. They are thoughts, not calls to action.

What you'll notice that will make this process much, much easier – for you is that the vast majority of the time you do not consciously 'do' your thinking, it just happens. It's a bit like when you put on the TV and of course there are lots of programs on but even with today's technology you did not put the TV shows there, they are just on. *But* if you engage with what's on, it affects you. Have you ever just popped the TV for background noise or company and then found yourself still sitting there an hour later and getting upset by the plight of the lesser spotted nearly extinct honest politician (maybe not), or found yourself caring whether some soap star you've never heard of, let alone met, is being cheated on by some other soap star you're never likely to meet either?

I'm sure you have; I think we all have; but put like that it sounds kind of ridiculous, doesn't it? Yet that's what we do every day when we engage with and react to our random thoughts without, well, without giving it a second thought.

So you pop the TV on and you're flicking through the channels, the news, click, the weather, click, the really annoying TV auction channel, big click just to make sure, horror movie, or is it? You sit and watch a little more, 'Yep, it's a horror movie all right and is that a guy in the shadows, what was that? A knife, oh god, and she's not seen him,' you want to call out to the woman walking down the dark alley, maybe you even do, and you sit paralysed with fear as she gets close to where the shadowy figure waits, ready to strike, the mist partially obscuring the object of death in his hand as he raises it to strike… OK enough, enough. You turn over; click, the migrating wildebeest running freely across the plain on their annual migration to… click! You see my point?

You didn't set out to get scared and you didn't expect it or see it coming, but it happened all the same. And whether it's on the TV or in your head, your brain will react just the same.

We are always filtering our present experience against our past experience, trying to make sense of our surroundings, and most of the time just making up the meaning as we go, telling ourselves stories and believing them.

You switch off the TV and go to bed, but wait, the wardrobe door's slightly open. 'I'm sure I closed it this morning.' You get into bed and turn out the light. 'What was that?' A noise you've never noticed before… 'Did I take the key out of the door? I did, ah good, but only after I'd been to the bathroom. What if someone snuck in earlier when I was in the bathroom and was hiding in the wardrobe and now they're…? Oh god, where are they? What was that noise? Oh god they must be under the bed, I want to get up but if I get up they'll grab my leg, oh sh*t I'm stuck and if I go to sleep they'll attack me.' All the time your mind's flashing from one thought to the next trying to make sense of what's going on, and all of it is complete nonsense… except of course for your heart racing, the sweats, high blood pressure and the fact that you can't sleep. And although it's very, very powerful, it's NOT even slightly real, it's 'just a thought' – just a scary story that the storyteller in your head is making up, and a perfect example of what we do to ourselves every single day in life… Until we learn *not* to, that is.

WHO'D HAVE THOUGHT IT?

So what I'd like you to do, at least for the rest of the day, is to allow yourself to become aware of your thoughts and to treat them as just *thoughts*, not as a call to action or a statement of fact or anything other than stories that the little storyteller in your head is making up for you. Sure, they might be true, but they may just be complete nonsense. You don't need to decide which yet! They are just stories, just thoughts, and you don't need to do anything with them except know they're not real.

Here's a tip and a trick that really helped me: every time I noticed that I was caught up in my thoughts, I would use the following little mantra: 'Ah, that's just a thought about...' such as, 'Ah, that's just a thought about being stressed' or 'Ah, that's just a thought about my deadline for this book.' And you know what? It totally takes the sting out of them.

What you are in effect doing is dissociating yourself – and your feelings – from the randomness of your thinking. You are making each thought a *nominalization*, a 'thing', and it's much, much easier to disengage with a 'thing' than with a thought that is presented as a fact, isn't it?

Sure, the thought may be true, but just as likely it isn't. What this is all about is giving you the freedom and choice to decide for yourself, or even better, to find out.

Break the habit of reacting to your thinking, and you'll automatically stop yourself from being pulled this way and that by any number of the 50,000 or so thoughts that we all have each day.

IT'S NOT ALL REAL, YOU JUST THINK IT IS

In effect, what you're doing would be like turning on the TV and assuming every programme is a documentary. That's what you do when you engage with and feel every random thought in your head. Remember, just because you think it doesn't make it true.

Can you imagine the freedom you are going to enjoy when you can just let those thoughts go and be able to choose exactly how YOU want to be in any given moment. When you'll be able to listen to your own wisdom instead of the clutter of your thoughts?

A CARING KICK – IN THE RIGHT DIRECTION

IT'S JUST A THOUGHT

Find a quiet place and close your eyes – OK, read this and *then* close your eyes. This is not the time for your 'to do' list; this is your time, your time just to allow thoughts to come to mind, acknowledge them for what they are, 'just thoughts', and then let them go.

So, with your eyes closed, allow thoughts to come to mind and just acknowledge each one as a thought about a thing: 'Ah, there's a thought about work' rather than 'Oh no, I forgot to do that, argh! I MUST do it tomorrow.' It's just a thought about work, acknowledge it and then let it go. This is not a time for doing anything and your thoughts do not mean anything, they are just thoughts, so just let them go… When the inside and the outside are not lined up, the resulting state of flux can only ever be temporary before your subconscious mind finds a way to put things back in order, one way or another.

Have you ever known anyone who's obsessed with money, yet as soon as they have any they find a way to get rid of it? Or someone who is constantly looking for Mr or Ms Right and yet screws up every relationship they are in? I think we all know at least one person like this…

I wonder how many people do the same thing in other situations: the thing that we perceive as being the source of our well-being is also the thing that hurts us. 'I know it's not right, but boy can it make me feel good' (briefly) or, 'I know I don't really want this, but the thought of losing it is even more painful.' Maybe one of these resonates with you…

AND…

Let's have another look at the source of our well-being and self-worth. Can you see the difference between 'I'm OK because I'm in a relationship' and 'I'm OK *and* I'm in a relationship'? Or between 'I'm OK because I'm a senior manager' and 'I'm OK *and* I'm a senior manager'? As I've said earlier, life is not an either/or equation. Our brains are far more clever than that.

There is one wonderful little word that makes this whole process easier – *and* you've just learned it.

And... the whole world may be going to hell around you...
and... you're still all right. 'My boss is stressing me out, the girl in
accounts is being a cow to me *and* I'm still all right.' And why are
you still all right? Because your experience of the *outside* world
and your *inside* world do NOT have to be connected.

We often see things as connected when they're not; it's just a
bad habit that we've learned – but also one we can break very
quickly.

How often do you wait for things to be calm or in harmony
before you give yourself permission to feel good? We attribute
things on the outside of us as being the source of that good
feeling, but actually it doesn't have to be like that. Our brains
can be far cleverer if we let them. Please get used to using that
one little word *and*. Cut yourself some slack that you are already
OK *and* everything else can be going on around you but it
does not have to affect your own happiness or well-being.

If you do it the other way round, you are far less likely to
actually get what you want. As my friend, the coach and
bestselling author Michael Neill, puts it: 'Happy people are
successful far more often than successful people are happy.'
When you attribute your happiness to being something that
happens *outside* you, as something that happens 'to' you
'because' of something else, you will always find yourself
trying to control that which cannot be controlled, and then
getting frustrated that you can't control it.

Then it gets worse.

WHAT'S RIGHT, RIGHT NOW?

You start to accept that the things on the outside cannot be controlled, so what happens next is that you start trying to change yourself in order to fit in, when actually deep inside you know it's not what you want anyway. But you perceive the pain of not having that thing, be it a relationship or a job or whatever, to be more painful than changing yourself and your dreams to adapt.

Have you considered that maybe the situation that's troubling you is just not right for you? And that if you were to press the 'pause' button right now, nothing bad would actually happen, despite stories to the contrary you might have told yourself? I thought not…

I'll also bet that whatever you have in your life that is causing you stress also has a sense of urgency. It does, right? Just ask yourself, is that a real urgency? In other words is it truly the 'if I don't put money in the bank by Friday someone will come and repossess my house' kind of urgency. Or are you just making it up? Is it a self-imposed urgency? A sort of 'Oh hell, I can't take much more of this, I need to get it sorted out and fast!' kind of urgency.

If the answer is the latter (which I very much hope it is), then that is not the voice of stress, that is the voice of action. And the only thing stopping you from listening to it and acting on it is fear. It's the fear that the pain of taking action is too great, or that the unknown is too scary.

No matter how painful your current situation is, the pain of the unknown can feel greater. This leads to a very 'stuck' feeling – but of course it doesn't have to.

It's a bit like when you have to take off an adhesive bandage. You know that you have to remove it because if you leave it too long even something which has previously helped to heal the cut will become dirty and infected and actually cause you more pain and take longer to heal. Yet faced with the very temporary discomfort of pulling it off you hesitate, pick at the edges as gently as you can, stopping when it hurts, until you finally pluck up the courage to just grab the corner and pull. Sure, it might hurt a little, but only for a few seconds and then the natural healing can continue.

Well, tough decisions in life are very much like that. We perceive the immediate discomfort to be far greater than it actually is, so we leave things alone to fester and cause us even more pain in the long run.

I am a firm believer that all things have a life cycle – relationships, jobs or anything else. For some things their life cycle will be longer than that of our physical body. Others will come and go, but almost certainly leave us with a lesson for us to take forward into the next phase of our lives. Every day's a school day and everything's a lesson, if you know how to look at it. Unless… you have attached your sense of self and your self-worth to the thing on the outside, in which case you are not just removing a protective dressing you are removing the very source of your healing or happiness and well-being.

I'd like you to think of this book as an emotional bandage. It's not the source of your change or your inspiration, just like the bandage is not the source of your healing, but it does create a protective and safe environment for your natural healing and change to happen.

Just like with the bandage, when it comes time to change, sure it might hurt a little, because change can be uncomfortable, but only for a short time.

Sure, it might sting a little when you remove that protection and use some of these techniques in the real world, but it won't sting for long and the results will be well worth it, I promise.

OVERCOMING THE FEAR OF THE FORGOTTEN TRUTH

I know it can be a scary thought, but you might just find that when you bite the bullet and get rid of the source of your immediate pain, your natural healing mechanism can kick in much faster than you could imagine.

It can be a bit daunting to head off the path you are on and back to the path of your true calling, but knowing and following your own path and your own way and truth is the only way to find your own happiness. I assure you that when you do, travelling along that path, your path, can be very easy. Almost like you are in your own flow of energy where things happen to you that you could not possibly have brought about through logic alone.

Do you remember my client from earlier, the one who'd split from her boyfriend and was struggling with her lack of choice and the source of her self-worth? The penny finally dropped for her when she began to reflect on the most productive and yet easiest period in her life, the time when it all just came together for her. But then – and this is when she got it – she began to reflect on the time just *before* that. You see, she had been in a situation that she knew was wrong for her but that she was scared to change.

She said that during that period it hadn't mattered how hard she'd worked or what she'd tried to do to reach her goals, nothing went her way, 'I just couldn't get it together, nothing worked.' She'd tried and tried, but even the slightest bit of progress was hard won and short lived. She was not definitely in flow then.

As soon as she'd removed the source of her unhappiness, though, not only did she feel the relief of the situation itself changing, something even more remarkable happened. All of her other projects and plans started to fall into place, too, and with little or no effort at all. One change opened up the space, and it all just clicked into place.

Have you ever noticed this for yourself? When you take the plunge, give yourself a break and step back towards your own path, suddenly lots of other good and seemingly unconnected things happen, too? The key is that the source of your happiness or unhappiness is not on the outside, not a thing or a person or a job title, it's very much within you.

Let me put it this way. What is it that you think will make you happy? Is it a new car, the perfect man or woman, a great job? Whatever your answer, ask yourself this now. What happens if you never get it? What happens if the promotion never comes, or you never find yourself sitting at the wheel of your own Bentley with Mr or Ms Right? Does that mean you have to be unhappy for ever? Of course not!

WHATEVER YOU COVET ONLY HAS THE POWER *YOU* GIVE IT

Of course it's true that you can be happy *and* have a Bentley, but I know plenty of people who have flash cars and are still unhappy, so it can't be the car that is the source of happiness (well, not for very long anyway).

It's the same with the way some people are scared of spiders and some people are not, and some people are scared of heights while others are not – so we know it can't be the spiders and heights themselves that are inherently scary.

Things, stuff on the outside of us, be they spiders or material possessions, or people for that matter, have only the attributes we *give* them. They have only the attributes that we project on to them. This is the same as saying they have only the power that we give them, and that is so true.

When we associate the source of our well-being as outside of us and go after that, we may well be heading further and further away from where we should really be. And the further we head in that direction, the worse the choices we tend to make.

I'm not saying that material things are bad, but I am saying is that making those things the *source* of your happiness, rather than nice to have as well as happiness, is the wrong way round.

THE SOURCE OF YOUR HAPPINESS

Let me put it like this. If you view a relationship (even though it might not be right for you) as being the source of your well-being, then you will do all you can to maintain that relationship, won't you? You will inevitably make choices not around what's right for you but around what is going to keep the relationship together.

Or in your job, if you view your position in the company as being the source of your self-worth, then you will do all you can to keep yourself in that position, possibly even if it means compromising on your own morals and beliefs and your true path.

I remember working with a client who had got himself into a terrible situation at work and actually got himself fired. He was an inherently good person but you could say that he loved his job a little too much and that was to be his downfall. Actually to be completely accurate it wasn't that he loved his job too much; he loved the way the position made him feel about himself, so much so that in order to maintain this he lost his moral compass and sense of right and wrong. Simply because the thought of not getting the result he was fixated on was far more painful than the thought of breaking the rules or even the resulting consequences.

As it turned out, and because he was so caught up in the immediate avoidance of a painful situation and so keen to hang on to the pleasure he associated with the position he held, he both lost the job and had to suffer the consequences, which far, far outweighed the pain he'd imagined would result from taking the risk of right action.

I was working with him to help him get his life back together after the wheels had fallen off. It was only when he had been forced to stop and think that he had the opportunity and the time to reflect on some of the choices he had made, and of course the consequences. You'll often hear people saying things like, 'I just don't know what I was thinking' or 'I was so up to my neck in the immediate situation that I lost sight of the big picture.' This is such a common thing; we get so caught up in the immediate gratification of either the avoidance of pain or the pursuit of pleasure that we lose sight of our true path and the source of our true happiness.

HOW CAN YOU GET WHAT YOU WANT BY DOING WHAT YOU WANT?

Have you ever found yourself in a situation where you know that you are doing the wrong thing, or the wrong thing for you, and yet you've gone through with it because your motivation has been somewhere else? I think we all have at some time in our lives and, you know, even though it might seem like you are getting what you want you are only ever moving further and further away from who you really are and where you should really be.

How many times have you heard stories of people being stopped in their tracks and being forced to take some time to reflect, maybe as a result of redundancy or illness or having a baby? And as soon as they slow down and let their minds drift away from the immediacy, they suddenly find that they really don't want to do what they had been flat out doing up until then.

You see, it doesn't take a lot of work or special techniques to take you back to your correct path. All you have to do is slow down long enough to listen to what your inner voice is telling you. Taking time to slow down and notice what you really want is one of the most powerful things you can do to change your life, and will have you living from your own true path sooner than you think. If it achieves nothing else I would like for this book to be the 'pause button' that slows you down enough for your own inner sense of knowing what to do to come to the fore again and guide you. I say come to the fore 'again' because it's nothing new, it's always been there, it's just that most of the time we are going too fast to even notice it. But I'm sure if you've not been on that path it can feel very unfamiliar at first...

A CARING KICK – IN THE RIGHT DIRECTION

Press the pause button (even just for the next five minutes) and take stock of all the things that feel the most 'immediate' to you.

Now, ask yourself this: are they really so urgent and present? What's the worst that could happen if they didn't happen? Be careful with your answer here, but just run off and make the best disaster movie you can, really be true and honest with yourself.

Next, ask yourself: what's the BEST that can happen if those things didn't happen? Take each in turn and notice what comes up for you. Often there is a very positive alternative if only you slow down long enough to notice it.

Lastly, for those things you are playing with, just ask yourself if they are fully congruent with the real you? That is to say, if you were being completely true to yourself, would you still do what you've been doing?

If the answer is 'No,' then I'd like you to think about this: how could you achieve the same goal *and* be true to yourself? Just take some time to think about that. If the goal is money, how could you make money *and* be true to you? If the goal is family, how could you have a happy family *and* be true to yourself? There's no hurry or immediate need to find the answer here, just having this type of filter will help you see the world very differently.

Don't get me wrong; I don't expect you to do this little exercise and change the habits of a lifetime, but it's another little step in the right direction. I know there can be something that is very familiar in doing what you know, and even if it's not right for you, and the thought of the unknown can feel quite scary and daunting… and that's where self-help books normally tell you to do something like 'just trust that everything will turn out just fine.' That's a lot of trust to put in something you've never done before (or not for a long time anyway)! And while I know from experience that this is actually true and good advice, it certainly doesn't always feel like it at the time, 'and' it only works if you allow it to by taking action to let yourself to get into flow. Only then can the universe, spirit or whatever you call it kick in and speed you along the easy way.

So if it's true that the source of your happiness lies not in the 'stuff' but in your 'stuffing' (the stuff on the inside of you), that's not to say that in order to be happy we have to do without the nice stuff on the outside. It's actually where that wonderful little word comes into play again… *and*. You can be happy *and* have nice stuff, but you can also have nice stuff *and* be unhappy. Happiness exists independently within you; the stuff is totally unrelated.

GETTING WHAT YOU WANT BY DOING WHAT YOU WANT

So, how do you break that association once and for all? How do you disconnect the stuff on the outside from the happiness on the inside? And how do you then accelerate your progress?

Let me share my take on how I try to live happily, day to day You see, most people make their daily goals things that are on the outside. You know the kind of thing: a successful day is one where they've ticked off all the things on their to-do list, or they've made their sales target, or their partner has picked their socks up and put them in the laundry basket for once.

The problem with these measures of 'success' is that you actually have very little control over any of them. And as I said, it isn't very sensible to attribute your ongoing happiness and well-being to something you have very little or no control over, is it? I'm very much in favour of only picking goals that I have at least some degree of control over, so this is what I do...

I know that if I am on my own path then good things will happen even if I don't often know how or from where. I know that if I am on my true path and happy then I don't have to worry about the hows and whys. Somehow things will just happen and in ways that are far more creative and effective than I could ever have planned or consciously bring into being. So what do I do? Do I just wander through life letting things happen to me? No, of course not!

It's what I try to control, or at least influence, that matters. I might not be able to really control many things outside of me, but I can diligently keep myself in the good place and in the good head space to allow all the good things to happen.

The source of my success is very much within me, and I am the one who can control it, every day. This can be very easy once you get the hang of it. The trick is to realize that keeping yourself in a good place should be your most fundamental daily goal.

The language I use with myself, and the meaning I give to things, is so important to my happiness and well-being. The way I treat myself affects the way I treat everything else I come into contact with… So what do I do about that? Well, I have learned that the route to success for me is not in vision boards and daily affirmations or specific goal-setting; my success comes from having a very clear purpose and direction and then allowing myself to be in a good, happy space where good things just happen. All I need to do is keep myself in that good, happy place and notice when positive opportunities are happening or just about to happen, then take the necessary action.

Imagine you are a singer, the front person in a very successful band. Now, as you'll know it takes a lot to put on a concert; tickets must be promoted and sold, the venue booked, the PA organized and set up, stewards to look after the crowd when they arrive and then people to cater for them and even someone to unblock the toilet if need be… But you are the singer, you are the focal point of the whole thing, so what is your responsibility? Is it to make sure the PA works? Or that the car park is staffed or even that the toilets are clean? No, of course not!

When the house lights go down and the music starts, your job is to sing. In order to do that you first must do whatever you need to make sure your voice is in good shape and that you are rested and ready to immerse yourself in the flow of the music and the performance.

Whatever is going on around you, your job is to make sure that you are good to sing. That is a discipline in itself, but that's what you must do in your life, in general… You must take care of the most important thing first – you.

That's what I urge you to try to do, every day. Your job is to do what you need to do to maintain your own sense of well-being. Do whatever you need to do to stay in that state of flow, and whatever you need to do to prevent yourself being pulled away from that place. If you do this, and you make your daily goal to nurture and support yourself regardless of what is going on around you, then you can only be following your true calling and advancing towards your true goals, and all with a greater ease than by doing it any other way.

Now I know this does not follow conventional wisdom, but what I have found over the years is that when I focus on me being OK I achieve far more than when I focus on doing and achieving things, no matter how important they 'should' be. Doing anything else is a bit like eating the goose that lays the golden eggs. The magic and the pleasure come when you are in flow and at your best. Your job is to stay in that space and stop eating away at yourself and the magic within you.

So how do you do this? The easy way, of course…

A CARING KICK – IN THE RIGHT DIRECTION

I'd like you to think for a second and give three answers to the following question: *What do I need to nurture me today?*

1..

2..

3..

Then, just so you are aware and on the lookout for them:
What are the things that might turn me outside in and pull me out of shape?

1..

2..

3..

And finally, for each of those, ask yourself: *What is the earliest warning that I'll get that I am being pulled outside in?*

1..

2..

3..

The rest is simple. If you know what to do, then make sure that you do it and do it daily. Not just when you feel good, if anything the less inclined you feel the more you need to look after yourself. And of course, when you spot the early signs that you are being pulled off track, STOP and reconnect to your own inner sense of knowing what's right.

It's that simple – which is not to say that it's easy, but it is very simple.

Your life will be shaped and defined by the values you covet and the stories you tell yourself, believe and act on.

Get clear on your true values, know what might pull you off track and then, when you notice that happening, STOP until you reconnect – because when you do, although the immediate action you have to take might not be easy, the alternative would be far worse in the long run. Then, once you are back in the state of flow, your job is to keep yourself there and, just like the singer in the band, your only job is to keep yourself there every day ready to perform and really live up to your full potential.

CHAPTER 4

ARE YOU A DUCK ON THE M6?

I have often said that I learn and take just as much inspiration from my clients as they do from me... And it's often said that we make some of biggest breakthroughs when we pay attention to the animal kingdom. But I certainly didn't expect to learn a profound lesson from a duck at a motorway service station.

Picture the scene, if you will. For some reason that seemed totally logical at the time, I had decided to drive the long trip from my home in Scotland to a Christmas party almost on the south coast of England, that's a good 450 miles and some 8 hours of hard driving (actually 7 hours, but don't tell the boys in blue). So, it was on the journey home on a very snowy night just before Christmas and with 800 miles of my round-trip behind me and the last leg requiring an extra shot of coffee for the driver that I pulled into the next motorway service station... These are usually soulless places and the natural habitat of the 'all-day breakfast', so-called because it really has been sitting there 'all day'...

But this place was different. Instead of the usual fast food and fruit machines, it had a farm shop and a fruit stall... Wow, great choice, well done me! But it was to be the next unexpected discovery that most impressed me... ducks. There was a duck pond, and although it was late at night the ducks were making a spirited attempt on the passing travellers with a kind of long-faced expectancy that only a duck can muster... I don't know how they do it or if it's just my imagination, but I swear that a hungry duck is one of the most persuasive creatures on earth. Anyway, in I went already thinking that maybe I could get a muffin and leave some for the ducks on the way out, just to appease the guilt I was feeling after crossing the feathery picket line outside. 'I wonder what kind they'd like best? Probably not chocolate, hmm, do ducks like chocolate? OK, maybe blueberry; that's got fruit in it so it'll be better for them.' Now, before you write to tell me that I've completely lost the plot, I know this is totally ridiculous! But hey, that's what goes on in my head sometimes. Go on, tell me you don't do things that are just as daft? Hmmm... Thought so!

Now, I think the people who owned the service station restaurant were in cahoots with the 'welcoming committee', because the huge panoramic windows look directly over the duck pond where the next wave of feathery muggers and are getting warmed up for their assault on the car park...

As I sat and enjoyed my coffee and picked at my muffin, I could feel all eyes outside watching and grudging my every bite... but my mind wandered away from my guilt long enough to think that these were possibly the smartest ducks in the world. They have a big pond, as big as my flat, and a ready supply of food which changes almost by the minute. If they don't fancy cheese, they need only wait a few minutes and the tuna sandwich crust will fly past their nose (sorry, beak). They've got it sorted, I thought; I want to come back as one of those ducks in my next life. But then, as I looked round the walls, the pictures reminded me where I was. If you drive 2 hours south from my home in Scotland you find yourself right in the middle of the Lake District. A place so beautiful it has inspired authors, poets and artists for centuries. Beatrix Potter lived here, and the village of Grasmere provided the inspiration and final resting place of the Poet Laureate William Wordsworth whose poem 'Daffodils' made the area famous around the world… 'The loveliest spot that man hath ever found!'

But I was not there; I was in a motorway rest area just beside the M6 nursing a cup of instant coffee which I hoped who propel me along the stretch of tarmac that would eventually take me home for Christmas… The real beauty of the Lakes was to be found just on the other side of the hill. Probably no more than a couple of miles as the crow flies… Or as the duck flies! And here is my point: my thoughts quickly changed from admiration to confusion. 'Wait a minute, duck nirvana is just over that hill, *and* they have wings, what the hell are they doing here?' Now, I know I've said that my feathered friends had a good little number going, but proper duck paradise was just over the hill. It would be a bit like settling for living right beside your local fast food drive-through when paradise was just round the corner, if only you'd bothered to look.

Now, I don't know if my ducks had an inferiority complex or whether they'd had a tough time coming out of the egg or whether they just had really crappy thoughts and internal dialogue, but why didn't they just take wing and pop over the hill to duck paradise? (Honestly this is the kind of thing I think about.) But it did lead me to a more important point.

WHAT STOPS US FROM LIVING THE LIFE OF OUR DREAMS?

Are you like those ducks? Do you even know what's just over your hill? As you begin to ponder that, let me gently guide you through the four areas that most commonly stop us (ducks included) from living the life of our dreams before we've even started.

1. Don't Know It's Even There

You only know what you know, and perhaps one of the things that keeps us most stuck is the lack of awareness of what we could have if only we knew how or where it could be found. Do you think your dreams actually exist somewhere?

Do you know that 'somewhere' could be closer than you think, or in fact could be right where you are if only you noticed and made a few small changes? So let's begin this little journey by thinking about what it is that you actually want.

Now, please don't fall into the trap of writing your goals based on what you think you can have. This is what most people do, but if you think about it logically it can only be restricted by your own limiting beliefs and experiences to date.

Think about it again. If you set your goals based on what you already think you can have, it's not really much of a goal, more of a path shaped by your current perspective on what's possible, which time alone could probably take you down. Someone once said 'a goal should be something that helps you to fall more deeply in love with your life.' Now, while that's a little too fluffy even for me, I totally get the point. A good goal is something that has a special energy to it, something that moves you inexplicably towards it without any effort. OK that's not quite true, a good goal will take effort, but not in the usual sense. It's the 'effortless effort' kind, as I'm sure you know by now.

How much effort would it take to go and collect your lottery winnings? How much effort does it take to travel home and away to follow your favourite team or to see the love of your life? It does require action and commitment, but you wouldn't really say it's 'an effort' Now that's a goal!

So, what might be just round the corner that would make you come alive if only you knew it was there? Let's find out what might be right under your nose waiting for you to notice…

I'd like you to pick the area of your life that you'd like to play with for now. It could be your love life, your job, your friendships, whatever it is that you'd like to enjoy more.

Now ask yourself, not what you can do to achieve what you think you can have, but what would make you come alive? What does your ideal career, relationship, friendship or whatever you are working with need to have in it? What does it have to do for you? What components do you need to have even if you don't know how they will be specifically lined up yet?

The same components arranged differently can have very different results, but the first step is for you to get very clear on what those components are that will effortlessly lead to your happiness.

Let me show you what I mean. If I chose 'career' as the area to work on, I might know that I need a career that allows me to travel, lets me feel like I make a difference, helps other people to feel better about themselves, indulges my ego a little and even makes me feel a little special sometimes, also one where I get direct feedback so that the part of me that has self-doubt gets the gratification it needs, that it allows me to make enough money to do the things I want to do in my life, oh and that there is opportunity to constantly learn and be creative.

Now that is my own list, but it could also be a rock star's, in fact it might be the same for lots of different people and professions but the basic components are the same. Just as we share 98% of our DNA with a halibut, these similar components can be arranged in very different ways and mean different things to different people… So, without thinking at all about the outcomes (specific job, specific person, specific people), what components do you need in your life to live the kind of life where your effort feels effortless?

So what else might stop our feathered friends living the life of their dreams?

2. Don't Think You Can

So, you know what you want. Well, you know the building blocks of what you want, and that's actually the most important thing… but once you have those, what might be the next thing that might stop you?

Well, one of the main things that keeps people stuck for absolutely no reason is simply a lack of belief that it might actually be possible. It's a well-worn example, but good none the less. In 1954 the world was gripped by the question: could a man break the 4-minute barrier for running a mile? Nowadays such an achievement is relatively common and even good club runners regularly eclipse the hallowed mark. But in the spring of 1954 it seemed impossible, until the night of 6th May, 1954, when three students, Chris Chattaway, Chris Brasher and Rodger Bannister, gathered at a cinder track in Oxford to prove the doubters wrong. That night they changed the limiting beliefs of most of the sporting world. When the clock stopped at 3 minutes 59.4 seconds, the history of sport was changed for ever. But, remarkable as this was, it was not the *most* remarkable thing to happen around that time. In the next two years, no fewer than 16 other athletes broke the same magic barrier.

A time which had been believed to be impossible to beat since man began to care about such things was achieved over and over again as soon as Bannister had proved it possible.

So had some new improved shoe been designed? No! Had drugs just been discovered in sport? No! Was that the year that gravity got a little bit less powerful? Of course not! But the earth had moved in terms of what people believed was possible. And as with all limiting beliefs, once they're broken they stay broken and can never be the same ever again.

As soon as you realize you can, you likely will… I'm not sure when the realization will come for you that you can have what you want, but as soon as it does, it's as good as yours, you just need to work through the steps…

3. Think You Can and Know It's There, But Don't Know How

I think this can be the most frustrating one. You 'suspect' you can do something and you know that it is there to be had, but you just don't know how to go about getting it for yourself. Even though it's frustrating in the extreme, it's also one of the quickest and easiest to change. It might even be that all you need to do is think a little differently.

The obvious answer to 'I don't know how' would be that you don't have enough knowledge, so you should go and do some research. I'm going to invite you to be a little different here and say that 'I don't know how' should always be followed with 'yet'. if you stay open to opportunity the 'how' will show up soon enough. Your job is to notice when it does.

Let me explain: it's not necessarily knowledge you are missing, it could just be that your approach lacks enough flexibility.

Let me introduce you to the three Rs of success. No, not the Reading, 'Riting and 'Rithmatic of our parents' and grandparents' generation, but the three Rs of today: right time, right place and right attitude.

You may have often heard that successful people are in the right place at the right time, the thing is when you have the third R well, right, you'll find yourself in the right place at the right time much more often, *and* you'll notice when you are. We're going to be working with these a lot from now on.

Right Time
Sure, you have to have an opportunity before you can take advantage of it, but you'll be amazed at the number of times this happens once you've got the next two parts sorted.

Right Place
It is highly unlikely that you will find anything new while looking in the same old places. If you've not found what you're looking for yet, how about expanding your horizon and your comfort zone and trying somewhere else? Now, it may well be true that when you change your approach you might just find that what you need is right under your nose, but

why take the chance? Why not start to explore all the other places your dreams might be hanging out waiting for you to turn up? I found that they were pleased to see me when I did eventually take the plunge. Gently, gently though.

At first I just started to go to different places and do different things. I began making new friends who were making choices I could only dream of, but the more I hung around with them the more opportunities seemed to be coming my way, too.

Now, at this stage we're not talking about the really big stuff (though it was big for me at the time). The clients I started attracting had more money and would pay more for my services – not that I charged more, but that was more about my limiting belief than their ability to pay – but I was being introduced to a whole new group of people. One guy I met wanted me to talk to his entire workforce about stress (well, stress relief actually) and he offered to pay more for one hour than I was used to making in a week! At that point I was still living in my home town and just doing a bit more travelling, which wasn't easy in the old car I had at the time. But the first snowflake of opportunity had landed and then another and another, and before long there were enough for a decent sized snowball that would, eventually and after lots and lots of effortless effort, begin to roll all by itself and gather its own momentum to bring me to where I am today, sitting writing this for you while very much enjoying the ride.

So you have to move house to be successful, then? No, of course you don't, but it might be an idea to start to think about how you could expand your opportunities, and think about what you could do differently. Where could you hang out to meet new and different people? What could you do to stretch your horizons and see a bigger picture? Who do you already know that, if only you spent more time with them or got to know them better, could unlock a new direction for you?

For now, just allow part of your brain to begin to ponder all the different places, people and opportunities you could explore. Don't let yourself become overwhelmed by the number of paths and opportunities that you might find. It'll all work out just fine.

Right, good. Now, the next part really is the difference that will make all the difference...

Right Attitude

The third R. Having the *right attitude* is like taking the blinkers off and allowing yourself to see what's been there all along if only you'd noticed.

The next time you find yourself in a new situation, ask yourself, what's the message for me here? What opportunity is there here for me? Now, sometimes the only opportunity will be the opportunity to make a new friend or even just share a smile. But – and it's a big but – sometimes however small it appears, it could be an opportunity to change your life.

It's funny, but even though we all have experienced this as being true, most of us remain closed to all the opportunities around us most of the time. Usually this is because we are focused on one path and one course of action, and have convinced ourselves that this MUST be the right way to go and the right thing to do.

If you are married or in a significant relationship, or if you have been in the past, I want you to think about the time when you first met, the very first moment you set eyes on that person… Now, had you woken up that morning with the intention of meeting the man or woman of your dreams? Had you set out with the fixed, focused goal that today was going to be the day when you found someone to share the rest of your life with? I'm guessing not, right? But were you open to it when it happened? Yes, of course. And then the rest is history.

Now, what do you think would happen if you spent more time in the state of being open to what might happen? More time in the state of mild curiosity as to what wonderful thing could come from an innocent remark or a chance meeting, that will take you down an entirely new path full of new opportunities and new choices? I'm betting your life would look very different if you did.

Can you see how that might work?

I wonder what opportunities are right under your nose, even right now, which you've just not allowed yourself to notice yet. I'll bet you actually know someone who knows someone with whom you could have a wonderful relationship, and I'll also bet you know someone who knows someone who has some work for you, and I'm sure you know someone who knows someone who you could help to make their dreams come true if only you knew them or were open to the opportunity.

Whichever situation you'd like to change in your life, think about it now. Ask yourself this very, very simple question: *If I didn't know any better, what would I do to change this situation?*

You can break this down in several ways:

- **What opportunities or resources do I have that maybe I haven't even noticed before?**
- **Who do I already know that could help me?**
- **What do I know but have never thought could help?**
- **What does the little voice of wisdom within tell me will help?**

Just answer each of those now and see what comes up for you. You almost certainly know and have many, many more resources than you ever thought you did.

The next and final obstacle to your success is often...

4. Think You Can and Know It's There But Fear What It Might Be Like Once You Get There.

'Death is not the biggest fear we have;
our biggest fear is taking the risk to be alive –
the risk to be alive and express what we really are.'
DON MIGUEL RUIZ

What is fear and where does it come from? Well, I'd like you to cast your mind back to the previous chapter. *We make it up.*

Whatever it is that you fear in the future, you're almost certainly just making it up and then believing the story you're telling yourself. I suggest that a quick way to stop being scared is to stop telling yourself scary stories.

The unknown can feel scary, but it's not real. You probably know that exact feeling I'm talking about. The flutter in your stomach, that vague discomfort when you get close to the edge of familiarity, that warning in your head that can be so easily misinterpreted as a red flag. You know what I mean?

Part of our mind always wants to keep us safe. It's a natural instinct that gets further trained and tuned throughout our lives to discern between what is OK and what might be dangerous. When you accidentally touched the hot stove or iron as a child, your safety centre learned from that. When you strayed too far from your parents and they called you back with that tone of worry and fear in their voices, the safety centre in your head heard it and learned. Unfortunately, most people's safety centres have gone a little too far in their learned generalizations. The lesson you probably internalized was 'If it's unfamiliar, it could be dangerous. Only trust the things you know.'

The result is that when you get too close to the edge of what's familiar, your brain sends off all the same warning signals and red flags that it would if you got too close to a hot stove. It's there to protect you, but it is also keeping you stuck in to a safe little place away from opportunity and growth, *and* it's not even real... you're making it up!

Some people can easily break through this imaginary barrier, ignore the warning signals and seek new opportunities. There can even be a rush of excitement associated with it that beats any drug. It's precisely that feeling of danger that provides that adrenaline rush. Unfortunately, most of us can't bring ourselves to fling ourselves headlong towards our waiting opportunities (or at least not very often) – but happily there is an alternative for the rest of us who are not happy to be stuck, but not impulsive enough to throw caution to the wind.

We have to *make the unfamiliar feel familiar*. That may sound strange, but it is very possible. It takes no money, no special skills, just a few minutes each day. The only thing you need for this simple technique is your imagination.

A CARING KICK – IN THE RIGHT DIRECTION

Sit down somewhere quiet for a few minutes (if you have children or a crazy schedule, you might have to do this in bed each evening, or even when you have a few minutes to yourself in the bathroom). Close your eyes and think about the thing that has been scaring you. Don't worry about the fear. In the privacy of your imagination, you are totally safe.

Imagine, step by step, doing the activity that has been giving you the flutters. At each step, stop and ask yourself what you are worried could go wrong at that point? How likely is it, really? And what could you do to avoid the problem?

What you are doing is looking around for the monsters and seeing if there really is any danger there. If you find a monster, check first if it's real or just 'could' be real if you choose to make it so.

Once that is out of the way, you can see the situation clearly for what it really is. Now you can imagine yourself taking all the positive steps to your goal, visualizing in vivid detail each bit as if you were actually doing it and totally free from all your imaginary monsters.

You can do this over and over again as many times as you need to until it becomes so familiar that there is simply no fear left; you might even get bored thinking about it. What you are doing is essentially extending your boundaries to include wherever you want to go. This is something you can do again and again, making your comfort area bigger and bigger to include anything and anywhere you wish. The biggest benefit is that rather than throwing yourself headlong out of your comfort zone and then discovering problems and 'monsters' that your mind had been creating once you have already committed yourself, you get to scope out the terrain bit by bit, and by the time you meet an obstacle (whether it's real or not) you will have seen it coming and already know exactly how to break its spell.

The important thing for you to realize is that whether it's a lack of awareness or self-belief that stops you or whether it's simply that you need a different approach or that you just need to stop making it up, the power to make the change you want is right there inside you right now.

YOU ALWAYS HAVE MORE CHOICE THAN YOU THINK

No matter how real the obstacle feels, you have the power right now to decide how you are going to get to the other side. You can decide to go round the problem by adopting a different approach; you can decide to reduce the size of the problem by challenging your negative beliefs. My personal preference is when we expand our awareness of what else might be possible if only we allowed ourselves to look at the world a little differently and stop making up what's stopping us.

If you're a duck at the service station, your biggest challenge might be how to get to the coach party before the sea gulls.

It's hard – after all they can swoop down and pluck your crust right out from under your beak. You might begin to tell yourself that you are inferior, or just not well equipped for the task. 'My legs are too short; I can't take off quickly and while it is cute, this little beak is really no match for the gulls in a scrap over a juicy crust.'

If you go down that route you will find all the evidence you need to feel stuck and trapped without choice; perhaps over time you'll even stop trying and just be content with the leftovers and whatever you can find later once all the other birds have had their pick.

You know that abundance does exist in the world, you've seen through the big glass windows and tried your best to wish things were different, to will that blueberry muffin over to you, but to no avail. But hey, at least you're not alone; you have lots of friends all in the same pond, so that must be your lot, right? That must be all that someone from your background and with your resources is good for, right? Best not get above your station, just be grateful for what you can get, it's a living… Maybe this sounds a little familiar?

However, you are forgetting a few things. You have all the resources you need to live the life of your dreams, even if you've not been using them very well so far.

If you just expanded your awareness you would realize that there is a big wide world of opportunity outside your pond and that the only barriers you have are in your mind. There are no real barriers, only the ones you create. And hey, even if there *were* real boundaries, you have wings! You can just go over them on your way to duck paradise… it's just over the hill if you want it. The only thing stopping you is… You!

That's not to say the journey will be short or easy, but why does it have to be? What would you rather have, a bit of a journey where you can enjoy the trip and a wonderful life that starts not when you get there but as soon as you leave, or more of the same again and again and again?

I know which I'd choose…

Find the first step to take on your journey to wherever you want to go… You don't need to know all the steps; you just need to know you want to take the first one. Go on, what's it going to be? What's the first thing that you actually want to do to take you towards your goal? Remember, it can be as little as you like, as long as it gets you going…

CHAPTER 5

DO YOU HAVE A GAY BOYFRIEND, TOO?

As I said earlier, life is shaped and defined by the values you covet and the stories you tell yourself. So I thought it might be useful and fun to explore this a bit and help you to become aware of where you might be holding yourself stuck, even though you don't mean to be.

The idea of our lives being shaped by the stories we tell ourselves was really brought to my awareness some years ago when I got a call from a client one day. She wanted to book a session to help her deal with the fact that she had just learned that her boyfriend was, in fact, gay.

Now this was not my normal speciality; this request was a little more 'niche' than I normally help with. But she was so distraught, her voice cracked and she held back the tears as we spoke, I just could not say no. 'Even If I can't do anything about the boyfriend I can at least help to ease the pain,' I thought.

The boyfriend was away working on an oilrig (a very male environment) for the next two weeks, and it was important to get her sorted out before he got back. We set up a session for as soon as I could manage, I think it might have even been the following day.

When she arrived at my office, every bit of my concern was validated by the look on her face and the tearstains that her hastily applied camouflage foundation just couldn't hide…

But as we spoke more and she sobbed, something didn't ring true – and the advice of one of my mentors rang in my ears: 'Never just believe your clients' he'd told me years before. 'Always check for yourself.'

Now, being a bit short on ways to check if her boyfriend was actually gay or not, I thought I'd just check how *she* knew that.

'Well', she choked 'we were out at the weekend; we'd gone out for dinner and then for drinks because he was going away. Dinner was lovely, but it was when we went to the pub that it happened.'

'What happened?' I have to confess I was starting to get really curious, perhaps even nosey, to find out what could have happened to convince her that her boyfriend was gay.

'We were at the bar, it was a big place with lots of different areas and it was really busy but we'd managed to find a table, anyway, we had finished our drinks, I don't normally drink wine but that night it was going down very easily and Joe (we'll call him Joe as I can't actually remember his name) had gone to the bar to get another round in. I could see him through the crowd and was just thinking how handsome he looked and how much I fancied him; he'd made a special effort to look nice and had even done his hair and worn the fitted shirt he knew I really liked on him... I thought I was such a lucky girl.'

As she choked back the tears she continued.

'And that's when it happened. I noticed that he was talking to someone, I couldn't see who but I got a tight knot of jealously in my chest. My last boyfriend had cheated on me. 'Who is she?' I thought as I strained to see through the throng of people. Then as the crowd moved slightly and the spaces between people lined up I got a clear view, and that's when I saw *him*! Joe was chatting to a guy, and he was clearly enjoying it, chatting to a guy, chatting 'up' a guy. I have always had my suspicions about him, after all, how many oil-workers use moisturizer? But as I watched the crowd moved again and I couldn't see them anymore. I kept looking and then stood up to get a better view – but they weren't there. They had gone. Where had they gone? My mind was racing, I felt sick. Where were they? Did he think I wouldn't notice if they snuck off together? Was that why he'd done his hair and worn the tight shirt?, It wasn't for me at all; it was to pick up some guy, and now they were who knows where doing god knows what and I was just supposed to sit there?... Well, as if that was going to happen. I picked up my bag and left! There was no way I was going to be treated like that! I went outside, jumped in a cab and went home. I have no problem with anyone being gay *but not my boyfriend*.'

Wow! She told the story so well (I guess she'd been rehearsing it in her head for a while) that for a second I almost went along with it. Her emotion was so strong that she almost carried me along with her.

But, as I say, I had the words 'Never just believe your clients' ringing in my ears. So I asked, 'What happened next?'

'Well, I went home but he kept calling me over and over, he just kept calling me so I switched my phone off and went to bed. Of course I couldn't sleep, the thoughts just kept running through my mind and the more I thought about it the more I realized that the evidence had been there all the time... I just wish I'd seen it sooner, I'm such an idiot, it's not like this hasn't happened to me before and now I guess I just need to get on with it and I need your help to get a handle on it before he comes back so that I can face him in a couple of weeks' time. Can you do that?'

Now of course I could, but the question remained in my head so I asked it: 'How do you *know* he's gay?'

'What do you mean? It's obvious; I've just explained it all to you. Which part of he was chatting up another man and then went off with him did you not understand?'

I like to think it was the stress talking and she didn't actually hate me, but in that moment I wasn't so sure. I decided that retreat was probably the best option, at least in the short term. 'OK, fair enough I've heard you, but have you considered that the story you've just told me might not be true?'

'No, of course not. Are you calling me a liar?'

'Well, no, of course not, but I am thinking that there might be another explanation...'

As we continued to talk, eventually I got her to see that almost everything she had told me 'could' be true, but just as easily it 'could' have been totally made up. Not through malice and not because she was stupid or anything like that, but because she might have put two and two together and come up with five... and a bit.

I got her to rewind and look at what had actually, definitely happened, and what she 'could' have made up: her boyfriend had gone to the bar to get them more drinks, he had spoken to another guy at the bar and then when she looked back she couldn't see them anymore... and that was all we knew for sure.

She thought for a bit and then said, 'Are you saying this is all my imagination?'

'Erm, not quite... It's a *product* of your recall memory and your imagination, and a perfect demonstration of the power of thought. Let me talk you through your story from another perspective... You were sitting in the bar paying attention to your thoughts (thinking that your boyfriend was looking hot) when you got a surprise (he was speaking to someone, which was bad enough in your mind, but then you got a second surprise when you realized he was speaking to a guy).

Then your brain had to give that some meaning, so – and I'm not guessing this because you said it – your brain went off and accessed the memory bank of previous experience and possible meanings and came up with 'he might be gay.' Then what happened is that you assumed that this was definitely true and then went off in your head again to find all the evidence that would contribute to this being true…'

'You mean I just talked myself into this state in my head?'

'Well, more or less yes, you probably made some pictures too…'

'But I tried not to think about it and it just wouldn't go away, and in the bar the feeling I felt was so strong… I can't just be making it up… can I?'

And there was my opportunity. 'How would it be if that thought wasn't true, how would it be if it was just a thought and nothing more? It's just an idea, but, because we like to be right we go off even further in our thinking and find evidence to support our thoughts. If you think about it now, I'm sure you can think of lots of times when you have thought of something and then gone off in your head and found evidence to support it. It can be as simple as *she looked away when she saw me, she must not like me*, or as complex as *he must be gay*.

'OK, I can see your point, but are you saying that I should just change the thought and think more positively?'

I could see in her face that she thought she'd got me and was just about to shoot me down in flames as soon as I agreed. 'NO! In my experience that doesn't work very well and especially not where there is emotion involved, which there always is.'

'Ah,' she said, 'so what are you saying? If I'm not supposed to think positively, what the hell should I do?'

'Let's look at it this way: what if the thought was just a thought? What if it wasn't real and the only power it had was the power you gave it? What if you were just getting caught up and then getting angry because of it?'

'Are you saying he might not be gay? That I might just be making it up?'

'Well, as I said earlier, more or less yes... What you might be doing is engaging with your thoughts, giving them meaning, and then feeling the emotion that goes with that meaning.'

'OK, I can see how that might be the case but, he really did meet a guy at the bar and leave with him.'

'Let me stop you there. He *did* talk to someone at the bar, and then you couldn't see them again – but that's *not* the same as "he left with the guy," is it?'

'Erm, no, I guess not. God, so what did happen that night? I was so caught up feeling angry and humiliated...'

'Can I suggest you ask him? Go and ask him and then call me and let me know.'

We did some work to help her to feel better and to further explain the idea that thoughts are just thoughts and it's the meaning we give them that gives them their power, and then off she went.

THE THING ABOUT 'THOUGHT'

Because *you* are the source of the thought, you very rarely question it. You know that if a stranger came up to you in the street and told you that your boyfriend was gay you'd almost certainly laugh it off, especially if the only evidence was seeing him chatting to someone at a bar, but when the thought is in your head it sounds like you and therefore it must be right. Right?

Let me put it another way... Imagine that you were in the cinema watching a very emotional film. What could make it more emotional? Well, how about if we made it about *you*? Narrated by... *you*? That would do it, wouldn't it?

Now, if you've never been aware of the power of thought until you picked up this book, then stay with me here...

You are (consciously at least) just a passive participant in your thinking, but you can *choose* which thoughts affect you and which you can just let go of.

So if thoughts are just thoughts, and you are just a passive participant, how is it that they are so powerful?

Well, the key is in the word *participant*. You are *participating* in something that you have no conscious control over, and that is the most stressful way to do anything. You are emotionally affected when you engage with thoughts but have no control over the outcome – and that can only ever lead to stress.

Have you ever known someone who gets really stressed watching their team play football? (Or any other sport, for that matter.) I know people whose whole week can be ruined if their team loses a game. Why? Because they are 100% emotionally invested in the result and have linked a large part of their good feelings and self-worth to the outcome of the game. Yet they have absolutely NO influence whatsoever over that outcome.

We've all seen people 200 meters from the action yelling at the pitch (or even at the TV), trying somehow to exert some influence over the game, trying to find some control and have their say in the outcome, and in the process somehow protect their emotional investment.

It's the same with the thoughts in your head. You have little or no scope to shape them – after all, how many times have you tried to replace a negative thought consciously with a positive one? How many times has it worked? I thought so… But you *do* have the choice of which thoughts you engage with. You can choose which film you want to watch.

Remember that whichever one you do engage with will affect you, so rather than trying to choose how you want to feel and trying to feel happy while watching a horror movie, just don't watch the horror movie in the first place. Doesn't that seem like an easier and far less stressful way to approach the world?

Now, I know what you're probably thinking: 'Chance would be a fine thing, but try living in the real world. Stressful things happen to me, that's a fact.' And of course you're right; things do happen – but it's your thoughts about the things that make them stressful.

YOU ARE IN CONTROL

If nothing has any meaning other than the meaning you give it, then *you are in control*. Of course things happen, but it's your thoughts about the things that trigger the emotion… Let me remind you of something mentioned earlier: 'Some people are scared of spiders and some people aren't, so there cannot be anything inherently scary about spiders.' The difference is in the thoughts people have *about* spiders. Just as some people find public speaking scary and some people love it, the difference is in the thoughts, not the thing. It's not the things that pull you out of shape, it's your thoughts about the things that maintain the tension and stop you springing back to the way you should be.

Now – and here's the twist – often the thoughts that bring the feelings either happen so quickly that you don't even notice them consciously (like with my client watching her boyfriend at the bar) or they actually happen completely subconsciously.

But all is not lost. The more awareness you bring to your thoughts, the more light you shine on them and the more obvious your thoughts will become and the more choice you have. Most people are almost completely unaware of the power and the role of their thoughts, even though you have thousands of them every day.

A CARING KICK – IN THE RIGHT DIRECTION

ARE YOU AWARE OF WHAT YOU'RE DOING TO YOURSELF?

One of the most powerful things you can do is simply to become aware of your thoughts.

Think back to our discussion in Chapter 3 about observing our own thoughts. For now I want you to notice when you are having a thought. Whatever it is, just notice when you are having one… This awareness in itself helps to make the whole process much more conscious and less emotional. Then, when you do notice one – and you'll get better at it the more you practise – just say to yourself, 'Ah, that's just a thought.' You don't have to do anything with it. 'Ah, that's just a thought' will be a great first step.

Of course I don't expect you to remember to do this all the time, but do try to notice and when you do just say 'Ah, that's just a thought.'

JUMPING TO CONFUSIONS

Anyway, back to my client. A couple of weeks passed and then one day I got a call from her. Her boyfriend had returned and she had indeed confronted him about what had happened that night.

As I'm sure you can imagine, it wasn't quite as simple as asking him. He had of course spent the time away listening and reacting to his own thoughts – after all, the last time he'd seen or heard from her was when he headed to the bar to get a drink. Of course in those two weeks his own thoughts had been running riot trying to make some meaning out of what had happened that night. Apparently they had ranged from 'Oh my god she's been abducted' – cue a phone call to the police – through 'Maybe she'd taken ill' – cue phone calls to all the local hospitals – and then to (believe it or not), 'Maybe she met someone else.' So when she eventually did make contact with him, it was perhaps not the most constructive of conversation ever:

'Ah, so you're back to me now that's he's dumped you, are you?'

'Well at least I'm not pretending to be straight!'

Confused, yes, I think they both were after that. So what really did happen that night?

Well, Joe, who will turn out to be our hero, had gone to the bar to get them both drinks. While he was standing at the bar, the guy in front of him ordered a beer and a glass of dry white wine. 'Sorry, we don't have any wine left, but I know the other bar downstairs does' said the barmaid. Joe, overhearing this, made some joke to the guy about women being awkward and why couldn't they just drink beer like guys do? So then Joe and this guy went off downstairs to the other bar in search of the elusive dry white wine for their respective girlfriends. Simple as that!

Obviously by the time our hero had returned he found he was on his own and a new group of people were sat at their table. He asked but no one had seen his girlfriend. Confused? I think so. He checked the bar, thought she might have gone to the ladies' room so waited there for a bit; he even asked one of the members of staff to go in and check to see if she was OK. His mind raced as to what could have happened, flashing around through all his 'emergency situation' and then 'relationship hell' memories at once. There was that time he'd left a girlfriend alone in a club for ten minutes only to find her, on his return, kissing someone else. Or the time another girlfriend had just stopped returning his calls, what had he done then? But none of that mattered now; she was gone, definitely not in the bar. He went outside and called her phone, it rang and rang and he tried and tried and then suddenly, straight to voice mail, the phone was off!

'Oh, god, something must have happened to her, why is her phone off?' thoughts raced around his head; he phoned the police and then the hospitals, and then finally thought, 'Wait, what if she went off with someone?' Again his mind flashed with thoughts. 'She was looking lovely, and wearing "that" dress. Actually, come to think of it, she wore that same dress the night she came home with me, so, oh god, she's gone off with someone else.'

I'm sure you get the idea… Can you see how it works? Now, I know that this is an extreme example, but I'll bet you a cup of coffee that you have been involved in something similar. Maybe not gay boyfriends and jumping immediately to the notion that your girlfriend would go home with the first random bloke she met, but I'll bet at some time you have got just as caught up in your thoughts and let them run away with you, feeling all the emotions that went with them and making bad choices as you went.

What do you think the quality of our hero's decision-making was like as he worried about what had happened to his girlfriend? Most likely terrible, and definitely not to be trusted. What do you think the decision-making of my client was like as she tried to make sense of why her boyfriend had disappeared with a man? Probably even worse. And neither of them had been remotely aware of what was really going on. All they could think of was that 'something' had happened that was making them feel bad, and they were trying to make some sense of it all and in doing so actually created a situation that wasn't even there. They were both just making it up.

A CARING KICK – IN THE RIGHT DIRECTION

Just think back now: what's the most ridiculously wrong you've been in your own head? When was the time you made up a story to make sense of something (we've all done it) and it couldn't have been further from the truth? I just want you to realize that we all do it and that it can put us a long way out of shape if we don't recognize it for what it is… *It's just a thought*.

Have you ever found yourself completely lost in your thoughts? I'm sure you have, perhaps on the commute to work, maybe on the tube or the bus when you just tune out the world and drift off into a daydream, or even if you are driving and you find yourself arriving at your destination but with absolutely no recollection of your journey. I think we've all done it, but where have we been? We've been lost in the world in our heads, the world of thought, the world where your internal storyteller is king and you are just a product of the stories it tells… You feel happy when the stories are happy – remember the time you drifted off into the daydream about your holiday? You feel sad when the stories are sad, and angry when the thoughts are angry, quick and harsh. I'm sure you get the idea: you feel the feeling in the moment just as powerfully as if you're really there – *but*, someone cuts you up and you have to break suddenly, or someone's phone goes off on the bus and suddenly you snap back into reality. You're not on the beach or in the meeting having it out with your boss, the feelings (good or bad) have gone in a heartbeat and you're very much back in the reality of your daily commute, and your thoughts, they were what they've always been, just thoughts that pass in the moment and are gone for ever.

As soon as you become aware that you are listening to a storyteller instead of being absorbed in the story, the spell is broken. Nothing else has changed, but the spell is broken... When you stop being absorbed in your thoughts and notice them just as just thoughts, the way you experience them is very different and will never be the same again.

HURRY UP AND TAKE YOUR TIME

Whether consciously or subconsciously, your thoughts dictate your feelings. But I'd like you to flip that round: if thoughts create feelings, then, inversely feelings are really good indicators of the quality of your thinking. You may not be consciously aware of your thoughts, but you are always aware of your feelings. Sometimes you feel down and you don't know why. That's because the thought that triggered the feeling on that occasion was subconscious and you weren't aware of it. But, since you are definitely aware of your feelings, how about doing it this way? How about looking at your feelings as a barometer of the quality of your thinking? Bad feelings mean there must be bad thoughts, good feelings mean there must be good thoughts, whether you're consciously aware of them or not.

So, the next time you are feeling bad, how about just detaching out of the situation and realizing that if you are feeling bad you *must* be thinking bad thoughts? And, given that your thoughts are not real, then you must be able to feel better.

It's funny, but often you don't actually have to do anything to change your mood. Just shining the light of awareness on your thoughts is often enough.

The other thing you might notice as a good barometer is that, the more urgent a situation feels and the more desperate you are to resolve it, the more you need to let go of the thought and slow down. Panic and desperation are just the feelings of worry and fear turned all the way up! The more desperate you feel, the poorer the quality of your thinking. **Do not** ever make important decisions when you are feeling like this. The more urgent a decision feels, the less I want you to make that choice. It can always wait until you are feeling better and, therefore, thinking better.

Please use this as a guide: *the worse you are feeling, the less you should be deciding.*

I really do mean this – although obviously I'm not encouraging you just to put things off, but please put off important decisions until you're feeling and therefore thinking better. When you are feeling bad, the action to take is not to try to resolve the situation; it's simply to do whatever you need to do to feel better.

I hope that's clear. The best thing you can do to resolve a stressful situation is perhaps a little counter-intuitive at first, but it will become obvious. The quickest way to resolve a stressful situation is to find a way to feel better, and then when you are feeling better (and therefore thinking better) you will be in a much better place to make good decisions about the situation.

YOU ALREADY KNOW WHAT YOU NEED

Even if it doesn't seem to make sense straight away, you do already know what you need.

Let me share another story with you now. Again it's another real story of a real client, and at first I thought this was one of the most bizarre things I would ever encounter in my therapy work. But now as I think about it I realize that the woman was doing exactly the right thing. She didn't logically reason it out, she just knew what she needed in that moment and followed her knowing…

I remember it very well; I was driving when I got a call from my assistant, Kat. She had just had a call from a woman who was, as she put it, 'unbelievably upset'. 'Why? What's wrong?' I asked. 'She has a spider phobia that she wants you to fix.'

'OK,' I said, 'but why is she so upset? While phobias can be terrible things, it's rare that I would get a call from someone so upset and urgent, 'I don't know, I couldn't really have a conversation with her but she needs you to go to her and so I've made an appointment for the day after tomorrow and will send you the address. I just wanted to let you know in case you bounced up full of the joys of spring like you usually do.' I thanked Kat and went on my journey, wondering why on earth the woman was so upset.

That morning I gathered my things together, including the 'pet' tarantula I had at the time (actually it was more a 'prop' or even an 'employee'). Rosie the tarantula was in fact my first employee, her salary of cockroaches and crickets hardly broke the bank… but anyway, she and I had cured plenty of spider phobias in our time. She was very comfortable and docile being handled and I think she enjoyed meeting new people.

I only once had a problem with her, nothing to do with a client but she escaped from her travel tank while it was sat on the passenger seat of my car and I was driving along the motorway. I glanced over to see if she was OK. Can you imagine my surprise when she was not in the tank but sitting on the headrest?

I quickly pulled over but, typical of Rosie, she thought I was playing with her and promptly scurried off and hid under the back seat. So there I am beside the motorway with a tarantula hiding under the back seat of my car and me on my hands and knees trying to coax her out without hurting her. Spiders have an exoskeleton (their skeleton is on the outside), so you can't really just pick them up, they're a bit like an egg, you could easily cause damage them if you try to grip them too hard.

I'm just glad the police didn't turn up – can you imagine what would have happened? Fortunately they didn't and Rosie eventually got bored of her game and came back out.

Never work with animals, even very small ones. Anyway, this day I got Rosie into her travel tank and made doubly sure the lid was on tight, and headed off to the address I'd been given.

I arrived and went to the door, leaving Rosie in the car (walking in with a tarantula under your arm is not the best way to make friends with a spider phobic) and it was just as well I had, as the woman was indeed very, very upset.

As we sat down in her living room, however, I got a sense that it wasn't just the spider phobia that was the problem. Sure enough, as we chatted the real problem became clear very quickly…

'Can you really fix it?' she sobbed.

'Yes, of course, but can I ask why it's so urgent now?'

'Well,' she said 'my husband used to get rid of any spiders in the house, but now he can't and I need to deal with them on my own. It's terrible and I just don't know how I'll cope!'

Part of my brain was wondering how many spiders she actually had in her house. The way she'd said it, it sounded like there must be loads every day, and I frankly couldn't remember the last time I'd even seen a spider in my house.

(Isn't it funny that we tend to have our sensor acuity turned all the way up so that we find what we're looking for? And often whether it's even there or not.) Anyway, the other part of my brain was wondering why her husband wasn't around anymore. Had he left her? Was he in hospital? Had she kicked him out?

'Do you mind if I ask why your husband can't help anymore?'

'Because he's dead! The selfish git's dead! And now I need to deal with them on my own.'

Before I could say anything else she went on, 'He killed himself, and now I'm left to deal with the spiders, do you understand?'

'I think so. I'm so sorry to hear that. Have the spiders been worrying you all this time?'

'All this time? It was only on Wednesday (the day she'd called my assistant). I came in and found him lying there' she said, pointing to the other end of the sofa I was sitting on. 'He was there and he was dead and now I need to deal with the spiders on my own.'

Wow! Now I could see the urgency… We chatted and chatted and I did my very best to help her with her shock and grief, and all the other emotions she was feeling, but the more we spoke the more I realized that the thing that was going to give her the biggest relief was actually exactly what she'd asked for. Far more dominant in her mind than anything else, more dominant than her grief, or whether she'd be able to afford to keep the house on her own, more than how the children would be without their father, was how awful it would be if she found a spider in the bath.

She reasoned that if she could be OK with that then she would be able to handle all the other things, and of course her own grief… So, what did we do? Well, I cancelled the rest of my day and we set about fixing her spider phobia once and for all. In between the various techniques we just sat and chatted (or so she thought) about 'stuff' and the principles of 'thought', and I guess that day I took her through the same journey you are on just now, but with a phobia cure mixed in.

She met and handled Rosie, and I am pleased to say that I left her feeling like she could handle whatever came her way (with 8 legs or fewer), not just then but for the rest of her life. After all, how could things ever be worse than the week she'd just been through?

From that lovely woman I learned something, too. I learned that sometimes the thing you most need to deal with is the thing that's right in front of you. Nothing else in the future matters if you can't get to it. If the thoughts in your head are pulling you out of shape, the most useful thing to do is to find a way to feel better. Then you can figure the rest out. And that's exactly what this woman and I did that day. By dealing with her spider phobia I enabled her to feel better, and once she was feeling better and thinking clearly she knew that she could figure the rest out for herself...

That part was comparatively easy. Once she was back in a good place, she was more than ready and able to tackle all the other things she knew were coming but would be easier if the immediate worry and fear were gone; only then she could think straight.

A CARING KICK – IN THE RIGHT DIRECTION

What's on your mind? What could you let go of now that would free up so much more?

Which thoughts and situations can you let go of right now so you can automatically feel better?

Maybe the situation will require you to take some kind of action. If it does and you don't immediately want to do it, then ask yourself 'What's stopping me?' As in an earlier exercise, ask yourself, 'Is this definitely true, or just a habitual made-up response?'

When you've got that, you can just let go and just get on with it...

What can you do (that you want to do) to set yourself free and take the action you know you need to take?

CHAPTER 6

WHY SPOCK MUST DIE

So, if thoughts are really powerful and we all have lots and lots of them every day, why have we not always been as confused and stressed as we are now?

Well, the answer to that is really quite simple: the more you engage with your thoughts, the more you get into the habit of engaging with your thoughts. In time it becomes second nature – but as with any habit, it has to be learned and only becomes a habit when it's easier to do than not do, or feels more natural to do than not do.

I have never smoked but I know plenty of people who have, and what every one of them tells me is that their first cigarette was horrible! They had to learn to like smoking, and then over time (and largely due to the addictive nature of nicotine) it became second nature, and so simply by doing it again and again the thing which once made them gag and wretch actually became a source of comfort and calm. Funny old thing, the brain…

Now, it doesn't matter if you have ever smoked or not, I'm sure you can see my point.

THE HABIT OF THINKING

So how did we get into the bad 'habit' of reacting to our thinking? Well, to answer that question we need to go right back to the beginning – to the beginning of you, that is.

My friend the great coach and author Michael Neill has a wonderful way of explaining this. If Michael will forgive me, I will paraphrase him a little here.

We are all born, happy, healthy, curious, loving and joyful. In his book *Super Coach*, Michael shares a story of visiting some friends who have just had a baby, and as he looks down at the little bundle of joy he gets to wondering how it is that someone can go from being so naturally in a state of bliss to being someone who, well, to be blunt, needs to go and see someone like Michael or me?

Then, as he gets to thinking, the first answer is the obvious one: 'Well, life hasn't happened to him yet. Of course this baby is happy, nothing's happened to him, he doesn't know any better.'

But because we understand how it works, we know that actually it's *not* the things that happen to us on the outside that affect us; it's our thoughts 'about' the things that happen to us that affect us. I know it's logical to associate our feelings with the things that happen, but that linear equation is just not true.

Think about it this way: it's easy to see how a child growing up can quickly come to attribute the source of their comfort as outside of them. If they dirty their nappy, mum or dad comes and makes them comfortable again by changing it. If they're hungry, again someone feeds them and they are comfortable again. Because we only tend to notice when something happens 'to' us, you can see how we could associate going from discomfort back to comfort as being external to us. We tend not really to notice our 'background comfort' – the one that's there in the first place and present all the time.

For example, we would all of us notice if we had a sore knee, right? But just notice now that you do *not* have a sore knee. Would you have noticed that unless I drew your attention to it? Probably not. Notice how you don't have a sore foot either, or toothache (unless of course you actually do, in which case I hope it gets better soon). If you do have a sore part it would be logical to form an association, a bond between you and whatever it is that takes the pain away.

I used work to work a lot in a dental clinic (don't worry, I was never allowed to play with the sharp things) but I do know that there are very few limits to what people will do to relieve the pain when they have toothache… I've seen many people quickly build up a very strong bond and association between the pill or the cream or the dentist as the absolute source of comfort. They're not!

Each of these may have the ability to take away the immediate pain, but the comfort is already there. Comfort is always there, waiting for your return.

Comfort is your natural state – so long as nothing is pulling you away from it. All the dentist or the pill is doing is 'resetting' you back to your natural state of comfort. And it's exactly the same with your thoughts.

PRESSING THE BIG RESET BUTTON IN YOUR HEAD

When we are talking about mental pain rather than physical pain, it is your thoughts and the meaning you give them that is causing you discomfort, not the thing on the outside. When you can break the habit of reacting to your thoughts – that is, giving meaning to those thoughts and then reacting to the meaning you've given them – you'll find the comfort right there waiting for you.

Over time, we get stretched and pulled out of shape by our ideas about who we think we 'should' be, what we think we 'should' be doing. We get pulled this way and that by the thoughts about the events in our lives.

Do you remember my spring story from earlier? We tend to allow ourselves to get stretched out of shape, to get pulled in different directions. The more we get pulled out of shape, the more tension and stress we feel in our lives. All the time, all our inner spring wants to do is to return to its natural state of being: relaxed, content, loving and just, well, happy. Remember, if a spring has been stretched and put under strain, you don't have to push it back into shape, you don't have to force it or struggle to get it back to normal, it doesn't take years of therapy or coaching, it just has an innate memory of who it is and what it looks like, and naturally wants to get back to that state.

Now let's take this idea a step further… what is it that pulls you out of shape? What is it that causes tension in 'your' spring?

A CARING KICK – IN THE RIGHT DIRECTION

GET CLEAR ON WHAT REALLY HOLDS YOU BACK

Quickly make a list of some of the things that cause you to be tense and stressed, the things that you feel are stopping you from being the healthy, happy person you are supposed to be. Just go with the first things that come up for you.

1...

2...

3...

Now, obviously I can't see your answers, but I'll bet you another cup of coffee (you can claim it later) that most of the items on your list are 'things', stuff outside of you.

When I first did this exercise many years ago, my answers looked something like this:

1   The location I live in
2   My burning desire to be successful
3   The thought that maybe I'm not good enough

I'm sure these are not the same as yours, but I'll bet there are certainly some similarities. It was in the last answer that I realized what had actually been keeping me in the place I was stuck at the time.

Conventional positive-thinking theory would probably have countered with some variation on 'Replace any negative thought with a positive one,' like 'maybe I'm not good enough – NO, I AM GREAT!' Or there's the NLP (neuro-linguistic programming) version: 'Take that negative thought and turn the sound all the way down.' Or perhaps the coaching version: 'What actions could you take to make yourself better?' All very valid ways of dealing with feeling 'not good enough', but for me the answer is bigger and simpler than that – and I'm going to share it with you now.

All of my answers were 'things' – and things that were very difficult for me to change, at that. What was actually stopping me from being the ME that I 'should' be? Thoughts. Just thoughts! My thoughts and the meanings that I was giving them were holding me in that place and preventing me from just springing back to the real me.

Let me show the subtext of my own list:

1   The location I live in – where I live matters; where I
    live says something negative about me; I 'should' be
    living somewhere else; I'm unhappy 'because' of this.
2   My burning desire to be successful – that I will be
    successful 'once' I have 'achieved' some specific
    thing; that success is a 'something'; that I'm not
    already successful; that I will gain something
    (happiness) from this 'success' – 'If' it ever happens...
3   The thought that maybe I'm not good enough – not
    good enough for what, exactly? To feel good about
    myself? That there is a point you can reach that is
    'good enough'; that not feeling satisfied with my skill
    level at this stage is a bad thing; that my self-worth is
    measured by my knowledge and skill level. That my
    self-worth is measured by the effect I can have on my
    clients and the results I get.

I didn't realize it at the time, but this last part was the
motivation strategy that I had used for many years. It worked,
but boy was it hard work – and led to one of my biggest 'Doh!'
moments ever. But you know what, they are all just stories.

I had learned new skills, and had got quite good at using
them. I'd even made the newspapers by being able to
cure conditions that had eluded everyone else. Those were
just the product of stories too, scary stories in the main.
I remember one woman who had been able to leave her
house on her own for the first time in 16 years when I cured

her agoraphobia, or the young guy would only ever eaten six foods in his entire life because of a phobia around food; within an hour he was eating anything he fancied. Not that I am in any way special, I had just really applied myself to learning, learning, learning what worked, and then refining my skills through practice over and over again. I got really good at changing how people viewed their own scary story.

All good stuff, and wow did it make me feel good about myself. The more I did and the more challenging the clients, the better I felt. It makes sense, right? And it was a great new story. *But…* it was a classic case of associating something *outside* me with the source of my own well-being. If the client got better, I felt great – but if I couldn't help I felt terrible. I also felt it was absolutely my responsibility to cure them, sometimes whether they wanted it or not! I had learned all these skills and had found a way to make myself feel really good… and a way to make myself feel really bad at the same time. Depending, of course, on which story I believed at the time.

What I was completely missing was the point. I had all these techniques and clever ways of helping everyone… except myself. I hadn't yet shut up my own storyteller or even realized that it was just that – just a story. What I should have done was, instead of using the techniques on other people and feeling good about the results, been smarter and used the techniques on myself to feel good about me. I know it sounds so obvious, but I just didn't see it at the time, not even a little bit. Often we miss what's right under our noses… Don't we?

But the real point, even at the time of writing the first version of this book, is that, sure, with techniques we can change our movie so that it doesn't affect us so much, but… it's still just a movie. It's just a product of thought, and our mind is trying to make sense of it… that's what it does. But it doesn't mean the movie is true!

The lightbulb moment didn't come until I was discussing the idea of 'thought' one day. The penny dropped when I realized that I had been engaging in the 'when I cure them I'll feel good' association and all the thoughts that went with that. Of course I now know I can feel good *and* help people, not that I feel good *because* I help people. The people still get help, but from my point of view it feels very different. Framing it in this way not only takes the pressure off completely, it also makes me far more effective because I don't fear the disappointment of possible failure.

Many thoughts and made-up associations lurked behind my reasons for being stuck, but as soon as I realized this and gained the awareness, the spell was broken and I could see things for what they really were: not real.

IS THE REAL WORLD REALLY JUST YOUR IMAGINATION?

Can you see that all of our thoughts 'could' be real, and feel very real if we choose to make them so, or they could just as easily be 'just thoughts' that can pass in a second and never bother us again?

If I give power to any one of my thoughts, I can feel very down and despondent, or very happy depending on the situation. Either way, it's my choice. Thoughts appear very real, and we can make them real by giving them power and taking actions based on them – but the thoughts themselves are just that: thoughts.

A CARING KICK – IN THE RIGHT DIRECTION

Revisit your list of things that you think are holding you back, and add all the thoughts and assumptions that are behind your answers. Notice what they are, and then for each in turn break the spell by jotting down if they're really real or just thoughts.

Now I'll bet you a refill of that coffee that your new list looks and feels quite different. How many were just thoughts that you've been making real? Now when you shine the light of awareness on them, you can quickly see them for what they are and what you thought was real is really just a thought. If you think back through your life, or even just the last week, how many times have you found yourself giving meaning to something that isn't true? OK, I'll grant you that it 'could' be true, but why act as if it's an absolute certainty?

We often do this, and not only do we make things up we often go off in our heads and find 'proof' for why what we've made up 'must' be true… It's not, and the quicker you learn to stop just believing yourself the quicker you will set yourself free to actually live from a place of peace and knowing and honesty… Honesty with yourself, that is.

I know you don't mean to, but one of my goals here is to help you to keep shining the light of awareness onto something that's been there all the time so that you can at first see it and then spot the pattern. When you do you will be able to do something about it. At first it will be conscious, but then over time and, just like the same process that got you there in the first place, something which at first felt a little odd or that you didn't quite get can very quickly become a habit and then like second nature. As with anything new, you have to go through the four steps of mastery:

Step 1 – You didn't know what you didn't know.
That is to say, you have been blissfully unaware of the link between thought, feeling and action (I say 'blissfully' with tongue firmly in cheek).

Step 2 – You become conscious of what you don't know.
That's the 'Oh, I've never thought about it like that before, hmmm, but yes, that does actually make sense' moment which I'm sure you've had already.

Step 3 – You begin to become conscious and aware of your thoughts and notice them for what they are.
Now, that's not to say that at first you will do anything with this new awareness, but very soon, if you keep being aware, then it will begin to become a habit – the habit of NOT reacting to your thoughts. And then you can get on to the next stage…

Step 4 – This is where all the awareness that you have brought to the subject really pays off and the idea 'settles' for you at a subconscious level.

This is when you just notice things being 'different' even if you don't logically or consciously know why...

Let's be honest here: you don't have to know why something works in order to be able to enjoy it from now on.

Remember, I want you to think of this not as something 'new' but as pressing the big 'reset' button in your head. We often make the mistake of believing that our thoughts of inadequacy and going down a path where we think we must find something outside of us, some magical formula or technique or piece of knowledge that will be the bit we are missing, the 'when I have that then I'll be happy', well, what if the only thing you are missing is 'the point'?

The point is, what if you *don't* need something new, what if you already have all you need inside you but you're just tuning in to the wrong channel?

Who would you be if you didn't have the habit of being pulled out of shape by your thoughts? Who would you be if you didn't react to the worry and fear? Who would you be if you didn't make things up and then live as if they were true? Who would you be if you could press that big reset button and put things back to the way they once were, the way they're supposed to be?

Who would you be then? Well, you'd definitely still be you, but I'll bet you'd be a very different you. Calmer? Probably. Happier? Almost certainly. More successful? That's almost inevitable... after all, you won't have to fight against all the stuff that's holding you back. And do you know that people following their path almost always find success? *And* – and this is the best bit – you don't have to DO or FIND anything new; you just have to allow things to go back to the way they used to be.

OK, I know it might have been a long time ago, but when that's actually your default setting it can be much easier than you think. Just like with my spring analogy, it doesn't take a great deal of effort or coaxing or determination to get your spring back... all you have to do is let go.

LEARNING FROM HISTORY

Let's just do a quick recap on the story so far, your story. If you just think back now, which choices would you have made differently if you'd navigated by your inner knowing instead of reacting to your thoughts? This is the time to be really honest with yourself.

If you had followed your knowing you might not be on the path you are on just now, or maybe you would, who knows? Whichever path you are on now, I know for sure that if you follow your knowing – and not your thinking – you will find yourself firmly on the right path for you.

Before we go on, I just want to be very clear about what I mean by the 'right' path. I do not mean 'right' in the sense that it therefore has a direct and equal opposite, which would be the wrong path. By 'right' I mean the guided path, the path of openness, the path where you are connected to and in touch with your inner guidance and can follow the 'right' path for you. Wherever that may take you, it'll be a wonderful place and it'll be exactly where you need to be in that moment. There is no right and wrong in the conventional sense, only what is now.

There is a famous Taoist story of a man who owned a beautiful mare which was praised far and wide. One day this beautiful horse disappeared. The people of his village offered sympathy to him for his great misfortune. The farmer listened and then said simply, 'That's just the way it is.'

A few days later the lost mare suddenly returned, followed by a beautiful wild stallion. The village congratulated the farmer for his good fortune, but again he simply said, 'That's just the way it is.'

Some time later, the man's only son, while riding the stallion, fell off and broke his leg. The village people once again expressed their sympathy at his misfortune. You've guessed it, he simply said: 'That's just the way it is.'

Soon thereafter, war broke out and the army recruiters came through the village on their way to battle, and all the young men of the village except the man's lame son were drafted and were killed in the ensuing conflict. The people of the village were amazed at the man's good luck. His son was the only young man left alive in the village. But again, despite all the turmoil, gains and losses, he gave the same reply: 'That's just the way it is.'

Whatever has happened until now has got you to this place; that's just the way it is… anything else is just the story you have been telling yourself about that and what it means. It's OK, you can stop doing that now and enjoy a much easier way to steer your own path.

LETTING GO OF FEAR THOUGHTS

Now, as you think about the idea of navigating by your inner knowing instead of logic and thoughts, just notice if this brings up any fear or anxiety for you? I know when I did this at first it brought up lots of fears like… 'Oh god, what if I've missed a huge opportunity by not even noticing it was there?' or 'But I like this part of my life and I wouldn't want to change that' or 'Hold on, if I'm supposed to navigate by my inner knowing, how do I know it's right? I mean, I'm not sure that I even have such a thing, maybe I don't, does everyone?' Those are all just thoughts, too…

When I really thought about it, and allowed the worries to pass, I realized that they really were all just thoughts. All of those fears were just thoughts which, if I engaged with them and gave them meaning, would take me off down a path. Do you see my point? I knew that if I engaged with the 'Oh crap, what if I've missed a huge opportunity by not even noticing it was there?' thought I could easily find myself feeling bad and stupid and beating myself up for being so blinkered. I could end up completely tangled up in 'what if I really could have had all those things that I really want but now I've missed my chance and I've heard it said that you only really get one big opportunity in life and I think I've missed it after all I am 35 now and so time is ticking on, in fact it's running out and I'll never be successful. I wonder if it was that job that I turned down? Was that the big one? Where would that have led, or should I have stopped that night and bought the lottery ticket? I know it was raining and I couldn't be bothered but maybe that was the night my numbers came and that'll never happen again, yes that must be it because I did have a feeling I should stop and yes, I remember now, why did the thought pop in my head as I drove past the shop,… oh god I'm so stupid… I'm such a loser!' Sound familiar at all?

I was 35 when I first wrote that. I'm now 40 and writing this revised version. Life has thrown some very tough challenges in the last five years, and some great joys and blessings too. That's always going to happen; that's just the way it is. But what I've learned is that the only thing you can really miss out on is now. No matter what you think, you cannot micromanage the big picture. Thoughts come and go, and you go on as before. Hold yourself and your thoughts lightly, and really enjoy just now…

I thought so. They're just all thoughts, just stuff your subconscious is making up. Yes, of course, they 'could' be true, the job 'could' have been wonderful (or not), and yes despite the odds you 'could' have won the lottery that night – but while these thoughts 'could' be true they're not 'definitely' true. Because they are our thoughts we tend to give them far more credence than they deserve. Part of the problem, as I've said before, is that our thoughts tend to sound just like us and because of that we tend to believe them and engage with them far more than they deserve. As with the gay boyfriend story, if a total stranger walked up to you in the street and said something like, 'You've missed the only opportunity you're ever going to get and now you have to be miserable for the rest of your life,' you'd probably dismiss them out of hand and more likely wonder which local hospital was missing a patient. Yet when we tell ourselves the same kind of thing, we tend to believe it.

DON'T BLINDLY BELIEVE YOURSELF

Please take note – just as I was advised not to just believe my clients, please DO NOT just believe your thinking. It's actually exactly the same thing, because often my clients are just verbalizing their thoughts and the products of their thoughts, and if I've learned not just to take them at face value, maybe you shouldn't either?

Please don't worry about the whole missed opportunity thing. There are many places you can join your own path. Trust that, wherever you do, it will be just the right place for you.

So, if your thoughts sound just like you and therefore, because you don't know any better, you trust them, how can you get to the place where you instinctively trust your inner knowing or innate wisdom, again?

YOU DO KNOW BEST

Let me help you to get there by taking you via the other place that people tend to take a wrong turn with this... When they first get the idea that thoughts are just thoughts and you can engage with them or not, they can often go to a place of 'OK, if I'm not going to engage with my subconscious thoughts I'll have to work everything out logically.' Hmmm... Now in my experience 'logic' tends not to be very useful a lot of the time, despite what Mr Spock might say... Just because something goes from A to B and makes 'logical' sense, doesn't necessarily mean it's the right thing for you to do.

In my book, logic is all very well and it certainly has its place, *but* we are all emotional, intuitive human beings, and surely it makes sense to use all of the resources at our disposal?

Think of it like this: if you had a job to do that required knocking in a nail, then I'd suggest you use a hammer or the closest thing to a hammer you can find. But if the job is navigating from A to B, then no matter how much logic you apply to the situation and no matter how hard you bang it, a hammer is not going to be much use.

But that's OK; you have other tools to use whether you realize it or not. Let's have a look at the other way, a way that, in my opinion, is the easiest and wisest way to be. I'm sure you actually already know it...

We have all had experiences of thinking of someone and then they call, or just having a feeling that we should go one way instead of the other, only to hear later on that there was an accident along our normal route. Coincidence? Hmmm... for a long time I would have said 'Yes' – but definitely not now. I have had too many experiences just like that to know that the other way works, it really works. It might not be logical or easy to explain, or even to put your finger on, but it works.

I have guided many clients to their goals using intuition and even sold my house for a great price in the middle of a recession when banks were going out of business every day and getting a mortgage was virtually impossible, just by navigating by my own intuition. As I've said before I'm in no way special, just showing you that this route can have some very real results, if you pay attention.

Was it coincidence that I drove past a sign for an estate agent and had a feeling to call them? Was it coincidence that they had just taken on a new client who was looking for a house in exactly my street, so much so that they would drive 30 miles on the weekend and walk around to see if there were any for sale? Yes, really!

Was it coincidence that they had just sold their much larger house and so didn't need to raise finance? Hmmm, I think not, so in the middle of the worst housing slump for a generation I sold my house for a profit to the first people who viewed it.

Now you could say I was just lucky (and yes, I was very fortunate), but I do think I played a part in how the events unfolded.

How about all the other things that happen to me almost daily? Like knowing to print off a copy of this very book the night before my laptop died. Yes, of course I had a backup on disk, but when the screen is just white a backup disk isn't much use. I was just going to bed after a day of typing and had a 'feeling' that I should press 'print'. I can't explain it but it saved my skin, because it meant I could continue working while the computer geniuses figured out how to bring my computer back to life. I hope we're both glad I listened to my little voice within that night?

As I said, I can't explain it, but I am still amazed at how this works every day, even with little things like knowing which way to go or even just knowing where I've left my keys. Is it always and consistently luck? I don't think so, and it's certainly not logical…

Believe me, I've not always been like this, the world is littered with keys and other stuff I've misplaced over the years… but when you slow down and actually listen, you already know far more than you think you know. You, too, can tune in to your inner innate knowing.

And here's the funny thing: when you stop thinking of such things as coincidence and start to navigate that way instead of just blindly following logic and crappy thoughts, not only do these 'coincidences' happen much more often, but you quickly realize that they are totally reliable and more trustworthy than anything else. If I can do it, anyone can.

Of course, the most powerful combination of all is the dynamic duo combination of the intuition of 'knowing' and the logic of 'learning' – but we'll talk about that more in the next chapter.

My intuition never gets it wrong. Sure, I get things wrong, but that's always when I stop listening to what I really know.

WHO ARE YOU TO DOUBT YOURSELF?

So, if we already know the answers, why don't we all follow our inner knowing all the time?

There are two reasons. First, it goes against our learned conditioning – it's just not logical, you cannot explain why something just 'feels' right (or wrong, for that matter), and all through life we tend to be conditioned to accept only those things we can explain and reason out.

'I just don't want to' or 'It doesn't feel right' are generally not accepted as valid reasons for not doing something , yet they're the clearest and most honest reasons you could give, even if you don't know why. Listening to and then following your inner wisdom is one of the, well, the wisest things you can ever do. Even though in conventional education we are taught to put little value on our intuition and instead focus on that which we can reason out, and through reasoning come to understand... This leads me to the second reason.

The second reason is simply that, because from an early age we learn to only navigate by what we can logically explain, we therefore have little experience of trusting our intuition. So when we do have the pang of knowing, we almost always test it against logic and see if it measures up and therefore can be trusted. Sometimes it does, and we call it a coincidence, but often it just doesn't stand up to logical scrutiny and so we dismiss it as nonsense. But what if it's actually the logic that's wrong?

What would have happened if you had taken the other path, the illogical, intuitive one? Where would you be if you had followed your gut feelings, your hunches, your inner knowing?

As you try this on for size now, just know that any fear that comes up for you is most probably the fear of losing the things you have and that you like and have formed in the assumption that you are in the best place you could possible be.

You probably *are* in the best place, given the choices you've made, but that's not to say you are in the best possible place you could be if you'd followed a different compass.

It reminds me of the story of the guy who dies and goes to heaven and St Peter is giving him the tour, and of course it's all wonderful but as they reach the end of the tour he notices that there is one door that they have skipped past. 'What's in there?' he asks St Peter. 'Oh, we can't go in there, it'll just upset you and we can't have that on your first day' St Peter answers. But the man persists and reluctantly St Peter pushes open the door and the man looks in bewilderment at a wonderful home and ideal family, just like he'd always dreamed of, in fact the room is full of all the things he dreamed of on earth but never achieved. 'Why didn't you want me to look in here?' he asks, 'This is the room of my dreams.' 'No,' says St Peter, 'this is the waiting room. This is all the things you should have had, even though you never thought you could, if only you'd followed the path that was meant for you. Maybe next time you'll know better…'

Can you imagine that, right now, despite all the good things I'm sure you do enjoy in your life, there might be a parallel path just waiting for you to step onto where things are even better? But it's not a logical path. It's a path where things come into your life that you could only dream of; where the only thing you have to do to stay on the path is to be you and be true to your inner knowing, and if you do that it'll carry you to your dreams faster than you could ever imagine. But – and it's a big but - in order to do that you must free yourself from the fear, free yourself from the confines of the logical world and learn to trust the power of your intuition, and not just the thoughts and logic in your head.

WHAT WOULD YOU DO IF YOU DIDN'T KNOW ANY BETTER?

Here I'm going to use a little logic against itself to help you get going now. Let's imagine that you had only just come across a new idea. You would not expect to just fully jump in trusting it fully and embracing that way for the rest of your life, would you?

No, I thought not... So let's play with it a little. Why don't you just test the theory and see what happens? After all, while you are testing it you will still have the opportunity to benefit from it, too. Maybe all you need are some new reference points so that you'll know when this new intuitive guide is lending you a helping hand, and you can only do that by staying open and in that space and simply getting to know it better. Very soon you'll know what's the intuitive gut feeling and what's just indigestion... that's not the same as your inner guide saying, 'Stay away from the chili next time...'

A CARING KICK – IN THE RIGHT DIRECTION

I hope you're up for this one, because I'd like you to spend the next 24 hours navigating just by your intuition. When you get a feeling, go with it.

If you come out of a building and think you should go right instead of left, do it and see what happens. Perhaps you'll bump into an old friend, or miss something that would have pulled you out of shape. Whatever it is that you feel your gut feeling is telling you, do that. Make a promise to yourself to follow it for the next 24 hours… You'll be amazed where it takes you.

Keep this to the little things at first, until you get comfortable with it. Then, once you have had some experience with it, some frame of reference for your intuition being correct, you can use it with bigger things…

Start by asking yourself this question: 'What would I do if I didn't know any better?' In other words, 'If I had no other frame of reference, what would I do? If I just had to choose without consciously thinking about it, what would I do?' Notice if that choice is different from the choice you feel you 'should' make. Can you see how that will take you down a very different path? Now of course it's up to you if you follow that or not, but I think it's useful even just getting an awareness of the existence of another path.

There is a saying: 'ignorance is bliss.' That's because you don't know any *better*, and so do what you want. Enlightenment is bliss because there is nothing better you want to know. The magic is not in what you call it, but in knowing and relaxing into trusting that you do already know best if you follow your inner all-knowing intuition.

You may have thought that logic was the only reliable way to decide where to go in life, but when you can see there is an alternative then perhaps you'll get curious as to what might be down that other path, and perhaps you might even begin to make some choices based just on your intuition and see where they take you… Of course, my advice would be to keep to the small stuff at first until you're comfortable, and then really go for it.

CHAPTER 7

WHAT DO YOU WANT?

I was really lucky growing up; my parents really didn't mind what I did… They absolutely loved me and they supported me, but they really didn't mind what I did when I 'grew up' so long as I was happy.

I was lucky that when the stork of opportunity was dropping babies off around the country, the one looking after the Lake District, where I was born, was a particularly keen judge of character. I couldn't have been blessed with two more loving people to call Mum and Dad.

I didn't always really understand that as I grew up, though; I guess we don't see what's right in front of us some of the time. As I get older I'm still guilty of that sometimes, but hey, that's another story altogether.

Growing up, I remember sometimes feeling a little hard done by watching other parents with their children. I knew that my parents were wonderful and kind, but growing up I wanted success! I was ambitious, determined and probably a right royal pain in the ass a lot of the time. At the same time, I knew that there were some parents who really couldn't care less, and I knew that was wrong and felt sorry for the children, what chance did they have? My dad was a social worker and my mum a nurse, so from a very early age I knew all about the sad and neglectful early beginnings some kids have.

One of my earliest memories is of being woken in the middle of the night, dressed and put in the car. My mum was working a night shift and my dad had been called out in an emergency to attend to a baby who'd been abandoned by its mother. In typical Campbell family style, if someone was in need, count us in, all of us...

The baby had been taken to the police station for a medical examination before being taken to a temporary foster home. Dad and I were to be her taxi ride to her new, if somewhat temporary, home. I remember the police cells, I remember the atmosphere and the feeling that bad things where close – not the police guys, they were wonderful with me, but I knew I didn't ever want to go back there. Maybe that's why I have always had a fundamental respect for the police. Anyway, we got the baby, put her in the car and drove off into the night. I was only about 6 years old but I vividly remember the scene at the care home: lots of happy, smiling children getting ready for bed.

Perhaps my memory has distorted the scene slightly over time, but I can still clearly bring to mind the warm glow of the happy kitchen, the hub of a warm family home and the loving care and attention immediately lavished on our little bundle of joy by the foster couple, true angels on this earth.

I will never know them again, but even at the age of 6 I knew those people were special. But not special enough to want to stay there… The thing that stands out most, and which my mum still teases me about, was that one of the little girls took my hand and said 'You can sleep in my bed.' I'm sure I might be slower to turn down the offer now, but that night I could not get back to my dad's side any quicker if my life had depended on it. Those people may have been wonderful, but I was going home with my dad…

My mum has since passed away, and reading the above just now brought a smile to my face and a tear to my eye. The lessons in this book helped me to deal with her passing, and to truly know that your world can be falling apart and you can still be OK. Really.

We are all a product of our personal experiences, our upbringing and our thoughts… these are the things that shape us all. Just be careful which ones you believe.

I was quite good at running, but as I've said I was mad keen on success and I wanted it fast – too fast as it would turn out. But that's when I wanted it, I wanted it there and then and I wasn't afraid to graft for it. I trained hard, was totally committed, I lived to run, it was my life and it was all that mattered. As I look back at it now, the ability to put one foot in front of the other fast was the absolute source of my self-worth. In fact, many times it was the only self-worth I felt I had.

I felt good because I could run, but if I couldn't validate that every day then I wasn't happy. I was one of those guys who had to break their previous time every time I put on my trainers; even if I was just on a training run I had to be faster than the day before. If I was at the track I would be furious with myself if I didn't improve on the previous session.

I know now that the human body just doesn't work like that, but even when my coach joked that I only had two speeds – flat out and physiotherapist's couch – I still didn't get it. I had talent but the completely wrong attitude; if anything I wanted it *too* much, I was totally emotionally invested and completely and constantly committed.

But not my parents. Or, rather, they were in their own way, they were always there with a lift to training, the right food and plenty of it, and of course money to pay for my much-needed physiotherapy… But, and although I know now that they had it spot on, their phrase 'win, lose or draw, we love you' used to really grate on me. Not just because I was a teenager and it felt a bit icky, but because the fiercely determined part of me wanted the kind of parents I saw at the track shouting and screaming, almost blowing their little Johnny along on the sheer hot air of their yelling. Surely that was commitment, they must have 'really' wanted their kids to do well.

My dad, by contrast, was super-reliable (in all the years I never missed a session through lack of transport), but when we got to the track he would just sit quietly in the café reading his book with a cup of coffee. It didn't matter how the session or the race had gone, he was just exactly the same, just Dad. At the time that attitude in itself used to wind me up a bit (like I said, I was a pain in the ass!). I wanted someone to shout at me when I'd run badly or to give me a clip round the ear if my start had been poor, but not my dad, he was just there... all the time just there, for me.

My commitment and single-minded focus would actually turn out to be the undoing of my promising athletics career, and believe me it was a painful but very valuable lesson.

Everything I had worked for, sweated and bled for over many years was gone in just a few seconds, and in less than glamorous circumstances, when I finished a really good training run at the track, crouched down to be sick and felt a pop and then a searing pain in my left knee. Although I didn't know it at the time, that 'pop' was the end of my running career.

Of course I did everything I could to get back to competition. I had surgery, I did my physiotherapy work diligently (hey, I'd had plenty of practice). I even remember getting out of hospital after one operation and doing two miles on my crutches because I just had to get back to training. Committed? I probably should have been... I really was nuts.

I know now, looking back, that the running path wasn't the right long-term one for me. It had been, for sure, and it had served its purpose and given me some self-esteem and self-worth when I most needed it in my life, but it was time to move on. Like I said, everything has a life cycle. I certainly didn't see it at the time, but it has turned out to be a blessing and I am stronger and wiser, if a little creakier in the mornings, as a result – and actually now I'm glad it did.

Of course, as we know, the thoughts you engage with and the actions you take are what shape and define your life, and for a while I engaged in the hard luck story… but then I got tired of being a 'former athlete' in my head, and allowed myself to connect with what I wanted to do next. When you do that, you are allowing yourself to step back into the flow and carry on with your journey, wonderfully supported by the energy of the people around you.

It's only in the latter years that I've come to realize how truly blessed I was to have such cool people in my life. Only recently have I realized that a lot of the things I take for granted in my approach to the world have come from my parents, and for that I give immense thanks, love and gratitude.

WHO DO YOU LIVE FOR?

By contrast, I've had friends whose parents took the very opposite approach in their 'caring'. I have friend who is a doctor, not because he wanted to be a doctor but because his father wanted him to be a doctor; the same for my friend who's a dentist and another who's lawyer. Others pursued the safe, sensible route which they thought they 'should' follow, even if they didn't exactly know what they wanted to do with their lives. I'm sure you know what I mean: good, safe qualifications. Two of my best friends did exactly that, but I'm pleased to say they're following their true happiness now, and can often be found teaching on the ski slopes around the world in between actually working for a living. All's nicely balanced, for now.

I'm sure you also know lots of people who have pursued the goals they thought they 'should'; maybe you're one of them?

There's often a huge difference between what you *really* want and what you think you *should* want.

I, for example, 'should' want to be rich and famous – that's what lots of people tell me I 'should' want. For me, though, the only thing money buys is freedom, and all I need is the ability to create as much wealth as it takes for me to be able to do the things I want to do to feel free, to support my wife, Claire, and hopefully one day our family. That's all I really want for us.

What I 'really' want is the feeling of security and freedom – and yes, of course, I'm working on it. But I don't strive for wealth beyond my wildest dreams; frankly, I wouldn't know what to do with it. My focus is not on squirreling money away in such quantities that I could never spend it; that would feel really hard and a very daunting task. My focus is on maintaining and nurturing me, so that I continue to be able to create the abundance I seek by following my own path. That way I can be happy *and* successful at the same time.

What I've found over time is that, one by one, all of my friends who went after the goal they 'should' have wanted or the goal that someone else wanted for them, are finding their way back to what they really want. It's the coolest thing to watch – and the current economic climate is actually helping…

SLOW DOWN, ESPECIALLY IF YOU THINK YOU SHOULD SPEED UP

You see, many of us sit in a space of fear: fear of losing what we have, even if what we have is not really what we want. At least we have it and we know where we stand, and if there is one thing we humans like, it's certainty.

Even when we're certain we're unhappy, at least we know where we stand. So, along comes an external factor like a big corporate restructure or a redundancy program, and suddenly someone else has taken the decision and freed us up to, perhaps, follow the path we really want.

With the right attitude and approach, even redundancy can provide real opportunities for following your true calling. Being forced to leave your job can be the kick up the ass you need get out of your rut (remember, a rut is just a grave with the ends knocked out) and consider roles you never would have previously, to discover where you could really be happiest.

Anyone forced to cope in harsh – or even just new and unfamiliar – conditions will tell you that the key to survival is the right attitude, belief and being flexible and able to adapt to your environment. Resiliently flexible, if you like? Trusting that it will all work out well while being totally committed, but with the flexibility to know that the present route might just be that, only the way for now, and having the awareness to spot the next move when it presents itself.

So now is your chance to sit back, take stock of your situation and consider where you really want to be heading. Are you following your path, or the path you think you 'should' want?

If you want things to be different it's time to really take stock of what you actually want. We are going to call on all the resources you have at your disposal, but, as you'd expect, we'll do it a little differently.

KNOWING BEATS LEARNING

Your resources can be neatly split into two categories: what you've 'learned' and what you 'know'. Now, before you say it, these are NOT the same thing.

Think of what you've 'learned' as the collection of facts you have gathered together during your time on the planet, all the facts, logic and reasoning. Then think of what you 'know' as being your gut feeling, your 'intuition' or just your own inner sense of knowing. The kind of thing you can't quite put your finger on or explain logically, but which sometimes you just 'know'.

Both of these resources are incredibly useful when it comes to making decisions, but one tends to get priority over the other. As we know, we tend to value logic and learned reasoning over intuition and 'knowing', but when you bring the two parts together, that's when the magic happens. That's when you can navigate your path with the kind of personal certainty you could previously only dream of.

Let me put it like this: think of your logical learning as your map of the world. All the things you have experienced are gathered together and arranged in a way that makes sense to you and represents the way you see the world being arranged. Not a bad way to find your way around, you might think, but, as with any map, it has edges. There are limits to what you know and, as with any map, there will be lots of generalizations – in the same way that hospitals are not actually an H but are represented that way on a map, for simplicity we do the same in our minds. We tend to group things together with other similar things to help us to understand them. Then, just like on a map, we also tend to distort things to make them fit with our expectations.

I was astonished the first time I looked at an A–Z of London and saw where the underground stations actually are in relation to each other; they are nowhere near where you would think from the tube map. It's the same with any map of anywhere in the world. And with our internal maps, we also generalize and distort things to make them fit our learned experience. Then, after we've generalized and distorted the picture, we delete information we don't think is useful. Even the more detailed A–Z maps don't include every street light, paving stone or set of traffic lights. It's exactly the same in your head: we delete any information we don't think we'll need, the problem is that we delete it first and find out if we need it later.

WHAT'S MISSING?

Pick a memory just now – a good one, one of your favourites. Then, as you let it come back, just notice: is there any sound in the memory? Or any smell? What were you wearing? Then just have a look around and notice what's *not* there.

It's worth just spending a moment or two doing this now. Pick a memory and, as you revisit it, just notice what's missing from the picture, if indeed you even have a picture?

So, let me ask you again: can this 'learned' and 'informative' map of the world be trusted on its own as a sound basis for your decisions? It's nowhere near as good as I'm sure you thought. At the very best it might be a guide, depending on the quality of the information you require. If you only need to know the sequence of the stations and their very rough relationship to each other, the tube map is fine, but if you actually had to navigate overground, the same map would be next to useless… Trust me I've tried and ended up getting a cab.

YOUR INNER COMPASS

So we know that a map is good, but only shows what you are looking for, what you know is there already. And it only allows you to plot the routes that you already have experience of. What if you want to get from A to B and you want to do it in a different way, your way? Or what if you want to go somewhere you have no previous experience of? What if there's no one to ask for directions, either? What do you do when all your external reference points are useless? Are you lost? No! You just need a different way of navigating. You don't need a map of learned experience; you need a compass. And the good news is that the compass is your inner knowing and intuition, already within you.

You already know the way; all you have to do is listen to the guidance that's already in you. A compass won't give you the detail like your map, but it will give you a consistent and reliable pointer in the right direction. Your own true north.

It's almost like a sixth sense, not in the sense of talking to dead people or receiving guidance from the other side – the guidance I am talking about comes right from the core of your being, the small voice within.

The jury is firmly out in my mind on where such direction comes from, or even what it's called. Some might call it spirit, others might call it the voice of god, and some use the terms 'intuition' or 'collective consciousness'. I often just call it a gut feeling or a hunch. To me it doesn't matter what it's called, it's at the very centre of my being and forms the centre of 'my' universe. It's the compass I have learned to navigate by and to trust above everything else.

Please don't get me wrong; it's not always been like this for me. In fact, had I read what I've just written a few years ago I would probably have dismissed it quickly and suggested a straitjacket might be appropriate! But that was before I learned to know better, and to trust what I had only had experienced fleetingly up until then. We've all had a sense of our own true north at some point, but that doesn't necessarily mean we've followed it through.

So how do how do you it, how do you tune in to your inner knowing? Simple, ask and then shut up!

ASK AND THEN SHUT UP

Close your eyes in a quite place, relax and then just ask the question you want the answer to. Then shut up and listen. You'll hear it all right. Even if it's not what you're expecting or wanting to hear, you'll get an answer anyway. It might take a little while, but then a really cool thing happens: the more you get used to tuning in to that inner sense of knowing, the more you come to trust it and the clearer you can hear what's been there all along.

Have you ever listened to a familiar piece of music and heard something new in it for the first time? I remember when I bought my first new car: I had specified the really good stereo and was looking forward to enjoying some of my favourite songs as I drove home from the dealership.

I plugged in my mp3 player and was enjoying just taking it all in – the sun glistening off the brand new gleaming black paintwork, and the feeling as the engine pushed me back in my seat when I accelerated, and then the sound, the engine and the exhausts combined to fill the cabin with a wonderfully melodic growl. But wait, what was that? It was a sort of annoying 'ting, ting' noise, and it sounded like it was coming from right behind my head. 'I don't believe it, I've only just bought the car and it's got an irritating noise already... argh!' As I continued to drive I turned down the stereo to hear the not-so-optional and very unwanted extra a bit better. 'Where did it go? 'Maybe it's only when I go over bumps?' Stereo back up and yes, there it was again. 'Bumps, that must be it.' Stereo down again and yes, you've guessed it, the noise went away. That was when the penny dropped and I realized there was a triangle in the background of the music I was listening to. I'd never heard that part before. It had been there all along but I had never heard it. Now I can't 'not' hear it; you could say I'm *tuned in* to it.

I often do that with music: I'll pick out an instrument and listen to it and only it, tuning out all the others (drums are always easiest for me).

A CARING KICK – IN THE RIGHT DIRECTION

I suggest, as an exercise, that the next time you're listening to music, put on one of your favourite tracks (something you know well) and then, first of all, listen for anything you've never heard before...

Next time, pick an instrument and really tune in to it. Tune out all the others as you do so. It'll really help your ability to turn your sensory acuity all the way up so you begin to notice and take in more of the information that's been there all along.

It's a lot like that with your intuition. You might not even notice it's there at the moment, but as soon as you do you'll never be able to not notice it ever again. In the same way, once you have an awareness of your inner knowing, you'll always be able to tune in to it whenever you want.

Now of course we all live in a very logical world, and I'm not suggesting that you approach everything with just a 'feeling' – but wouldn't it be useful to have a warning system or something that you could check in with when you're not sure what to do? That's exactly what I'm suggesting: a way of knowing if you are on your path and, if not, which direction can take you back there quickest.

Well you do and that's exactly what I want to help you to 'tune up'. You see, my intuition isn't something that I'm aware of all the time; it's something that I can either check in with or that will alert me if I should be checking in with it.

I only ever go wrong if I stop listening or if I can't be bothered to act on it. As I said earlier, sometimes we don't like what our inner knowing is it's telling us and think we know better or think that somehow we manipulate or change or control that situation so that we do get what we want but I assure you that's just the thoughts in your head playing tricks on you and has nothing to do with it being the right path. If in doubt, ask, on the inside, then shut up and listen!

Of course logic has its place and doesn't just fall by the wayside, remember I said that the magic comes when you blend what you've 'learned' with what you 'know'. It is this balance you need to practise and get familiar with.

You have learned what you have learned, and of course even if you can't recall everything you've absorbed over the years you have been shaped by it just the same, and like it or not you're the person you are because of having absorbed all of that information and those experiences.

YOU'RE NOT REALLY STUCK

Let me be really clear here: if you are feeling stuck because of a lack of learning or information, you're not really stuck at all. Just take action and go and find out. If it's just information you're lacking, then despite what you might be telling yourself you're not really stuck, information has never been more readily available… it's right at your fingertips. If you want to know the capital of Albania or its population or anything else no matter how obscure, just go find out.

While in the past it might have been true that the lack of information could hold you back, it's just not true anymore, you can almost certainly find out in just a few clicks… (Oh and the answers are Tirana and 3.5 million, by the way). So we can safely assume that there is nothing wrong with the information you have available; your map of the world can be checked, tested and expanded as and when required with very little effort at all. Which, therefore, brings us to the other part, the part that must be present for the real magic to happen: your inner knowing.

LISTEN TO YOUR INNER KNOWING

Have you ever got out of your car and been just about to shut the door when a little voice in your head tells you to check you've got the key? Have you ever met someone and just had a 'feeling' about him or her? Have you ever just had a hunch, or a gut feeling about something? We all have, but how many times do you listen to these 'knowings'? I'll bet it's not as often as you should, if at all. But when you *do* listen, how often is your hunch right? I think you'll find that it's the vast majority of the time. So why don't you listen to it more?

Well, the first reason is that, as I've said before, we are conditioned to value logic more than feeling. After all, it does sound a bit silly to say, 'It just doesn't feel right' in the boardroom with nothing else to back you up – but do you know what? I trust my gut feeling far more than logic now. I have travelled halfway round the world because I've had a 'feeling' that, if I did, something amazing would happen – and of course it did. I have not locked myself out or lost my wallet (touch wood) in a very long time, and I have made some very different decisions than I would have if I had been making them logically.

Getting to the point where you can trust and just check in with your intuition takes time and practice, but you'll be surprised at how quickly you can tune in to it when you allow yourself.

A CARING KICK – IN THE RIGHT DIRECTION

Let's do a little experiment now to test your intuition. I'd like you to close your eyes (OK, as before, read this and then close your eyes) and think of a time you made a good decision.

When you've thought of one make the picture in your mind big and bright and bold. Allow the memory to come back fully. Now go back to just before you made the decision; go back to the time when you knew the decision you were going to make and knew it was the right one.

Sit and enjoy that good feeling and, as you do, ask yourself this: 'How did I know it was going to be the right decision?'

What did it feel like? What is it *inside of you* that lets you know when it's the right decision? Just notice this now. You might have to do it a few times to get the hang of it, but if you have the time and space to do so, do that a few times just now.

Cool. Now I'd like you to repeat the exercise, but this time think of a time when you made a bad decision. Close your eyes and go back to the memory of a bad decision. Before you do, though, I'd like to qualify what I'm asking you to do here, and advise you that this is not the time to try to deal with anything above a 5 on an emotional scale from 1 – 10. You'll be able to work through the big stuff in time, but for now I just want to help you to tune in a little.

Right, that's the health warning out of the way, so just read this and then close your eyes and go back in your memory to a time when you made a bad decision. When you've got one, go back a little further to just before you made that decision. Ask yourself: 'Did I know it was a bad decision'? Even if you didn't want to listen to the small warning voice within, it's incredibly likely that you did already know it was wrong. You did, didn't you?

AWARENESS

That's not to say it's easy to make the right decision all the time, but being aware is the first step. I have worked with many people who have told me a variation on, 'I knew I shouldn't have married her' or 'I knew it was the wrong thing to do but it was just too painful to pull out.' I'm sure you'll have had an experience just like that – obviously I don't just mean a bad marriage, but we've all of us gone down a route that we 'knew' was wrong for us, and yet the pain of turning back just seemed and felt too great. Well, here's my learning: no matter how painful it seems to change course, the pain of carrying on down the wrong path is always going to be much greater in the long term.

If you are ever in doubt, side with your 'knowing'. It's a far better judge than anything else you'll have in that moment, and once you have got used to trusting it and tuning in to it, you will find it so much easier to rely on – even to the point where you just don't question it anymore, even when it surprises you.

If in doubt about what to do in any situation, ask yourself: 'If I didn't know any better, what would I do next'? Then listen for the answer. Even if part of you doesn't like the answer that comes your way. In order to set yourself free and fully navigate the right path for you, you must also give up on your attachment to the outcome. Remember that the outcome you desire is only the best you can conceive based on what you have learned to date; it might not be the best outcome for you. All pain comes from attachment. It's this attachment to a specific outcome that can easily steer you off down the wrong path. But, as I've said before, the real magic comes in combining learning and knowing. Here's how I do it now, and how I help my clients to get some very big breakthroughs very easily.

CHECK IN WITH YOUR INTUITION, THEN CHECK IT OUT WITH LOGIC

Go to your compass first, then check that against your map. That is to say, check in with your intuition first and then check it out with your learning. It's amazing the difference that doing it this way round makes. Check your intuition, then check your facts. It's probably the kind of thing you already do, only turned on its head: in the conventional way, once you have had a thought and have made a decision, you have stopped being fluid and flexible. You have laid down a marker and part of your brain goes off and finds all the evidence it can to back it up, to make you right, even when you're not. Now you can use this natural habit in your favour, if you turn it upside down.

Check in with your knowing first, and then check if that could be true, even if you have no experience of it yet. Then all you have to do next is follow through and follow your wisdom.

If you start too big this might not be so easy, so for now I'd love it if you would just play with the very small things until you get used to this new way of being.

Pick something small that you would like to change, something that doesn't 'really' matter, that you can play with. Ask: 'If I didn't know any better, what would I do next?' Then ask: 'Why is that a good idea'? And, without over-analysing it, go and act on the answer, then notice how it works out. Once you get the hang of this you will be able to make bigger choices this way, but for now keep it to baby steps.

Once you get going and find your feet, you can really start to run with this. At that point you can change the question to: 'If

I didn't know any better, what would I want next?' And then: 'If I didn't know any better, what would the right path be for me?' Remember to check in with your map: 'Why is that a good idea?'

The key to finding the right path for you is to find, and stay, on the one that fulfils both parts: the logical and the 'knowing'. And of course the easiest way to do this is to use these parts to find your path in the first place.

A CARING KICK – IN THE RIGHT DIRECTION

Answer this question: 'If I didn't know any better, what would I do next?' Then just notice what comes up for you… why do you know that's a good idea? And again notice what comes up… isn't this already getting easier?

It's the funniest thing: when it clicks, even if you don't know why, something can shift on the inside and it can feel like coming home, or putting on a favourite old pair of jeans (why are jeans always at their best just before you have to throw them out? One of life's cruel tricks). But when you get the balance right between using your compass of intuition and checking it against your map of logic, you will find that things can get easier than you can imagine. That's how you'll be able to navigate the course you really want, because when you do that the rest is easy and you'll never want for motivation again.

If you're on a path and lacking motivation and feeling like you just don't want to do something, maybe there's nothing wrong with your motivation; maybe you really just don't want to do it, you've just got the wrong goal or are on the wrong path... Real support doesn't come from yelling (inside your head or outside), it comes when you create a nurturing environment and steer a true course where you are OK and doing what you really want to do. It can be that simple and easy.

Oh, one small point: remember that what you have learned logically may not actually even be correct. We are all guilty of storing up facts that might not be quite right even if we believe them to be. If you find yourself not being able to 'fit' your intuition to your reasoning, it's well worth just checking your facts in case they're wrong. Even with the best intentions, it may well be the case and I'd hate you to go back to doubting your intuition when it's your facts you need to get straight.

Put simply, north is always north, but maps can easily be wrong or out of date. It's worth checking before you head off... Follow your own true north.

Have fun – and remember, success is a journey, not a destination. Enjoy yours... now!

CHAPTER 8

ARE YOU READY TO MAKE A DIFFERENCE?

So you want things to be different? But are you really up for doing what it takes?

Everything you have done so far has brought you to this point, but if you want change in your life you are going to have to do some changing first.

Are you ready to give life a shot and move past fear, limiting belief and previous experience to go after what you want and create the reality you really want to live? If you are, then you are now in exactly the right place. But before you can do this, it's time to check in with your map and see where you would like to be, even if you don't know how you're going to get there.

Here's a tip: I know that lots of other self-help people talk about making goals specific and measurable; well, I would suggest that doing it that way is the old outside-in, logical approach, so I'm going to encourage you to do it differently. Instead of setting a goal of 'I want a sports car,' think about what owning a sports car would mean to you. How would it make you feel? What thoughts would it bring up, what would you be able to check in with that would let you know you're OK once you had a flash sports car parked in the driveway? Would it be, 'I'm successful in a way that everyone can see?' or, 'I'd feel like I'd achieved something really cool and I'd be able to check in with the fact that, in order to have a sports car, I'd know that I am capable of creating far more than the cost of the car – after all I'm not likely to spend "every" penny I had on a sports car.' So in this case why not make 'feeling successful in an obvious way' or 'knowing and having evidence of being able to create and be abundant' your goals? Tune in to the feelings and inner knowing, the rest will take care of itself.

Those would be far clearer goals and much more powerful than 'owing a sports car', the *thing* goal is a symbol of powerful inner achievement, so it might be represented on your map by the symbol of a particular sports car. It's nothing more than that: just a symbol of something else and not definitely something to attach your self-worth to or to which you should be enslaved in the pursuit of. Remember, just like a hospital is represented by an H but doesn't look anything like one in real life, your powerful inner goals can be represented by symbols of whatever *things* you like, so long as they have meaning for you and you have the key (to the map, not the car). I'd actually bet that when you get to the point when you can own a sports car you choose not to, but that's another story entirely. Just knowing you can is probably enough to feel really good, whether or not you actually go ahead and do so!

So that's the map part: think of what it is that you want, and then look a bit deeper for the powerful inner goals, the ones that are going to propel you effortlessly forward. All you have to do then is steer the course.

And that's where the compass of your inner knowing comes in very useful. You don't need to know all the steps you're going to take on your journey when you set out. As with any journey, of course there are going to be detours, and hold-ups, but hopefully a few shortcuts along the way, too. The key to finding the shortcuts – and indeed to staying on the right path and in your own flow – is to follow the compass of your inner knowing.

While the map is firmly on the outside in the features of the world around you, your compass is on the inside and, just like the invisible magnetic pull that always points a compass needle north, your compass of intuition is just as strong and every bit as reliable… When you let it.

And that's the next point. If you've not done so already, it's definitely time to start tuning in to your inner knowing and playing with it until you know to trust it… Please do as I said before: this book has a far better chance of helping you if you actually practise the exercises. While I'm hoping that you are enjoying reading it, I know you'll enjoy the results of your efforts a whole lot more. Tune in to your inner knowing; it'll make all the difference to you because that really is all you need to keep on the path that's right for you. And although that path will have bumps and obstacles, too, I can't emphasize how much easier it will be than any other way.

STOP BATTLING AGAINST THE CURRENT

I like to think about it this way: when I'm in flow and following my inner knowing it's like being in a boat flowing effortlessly downstream. If I want to go faster I can paddle and get there and bit quicker, or I can just enjoy the ride and steer the course. There'll be the odd rock and rough bit, but as long as I stay in the boat and keep steering with my intuition I'll get there. If I want it can be that easy, so long as I know where 'there' is – but that's what my map's for.

Then there is the other way, perhaps the way you've been using until now? You're in the boat but you're going upstream, battling against the forces of nature and having to fight and struggle all the way. While there might well be something nice upstream that you think is worthwhile, have a think about this: what if you've always been on this journey down river, and the thing you're battling so hard to get upstream for is something you have passed by, and that you should have passed by? But maybe as you passed by it caught your attention, you had some thoughts about it and gave them some meaning, which may well have even been true at some point but are maybe not true now. You've moved on from there and now you're a bit further downstream, but you still have that attachment and you still want to go back, you still have the same thoughts and so you keep paddling and paddling until you either get there, exhausted, or give up.

Sound familiar?

Now think, what if there's been something even better downstream all along? What if that thing you've been battling against nature for is not the best you can do or have? What if the force of nature you've been fighting against is the fact that it's not right for you and your inner wisdom knows that and is trying not to let you make a mistake by going there?

It may well just be that the thing you are transfixed on might not be the best outcome for you. I use the word 'transfixed' deliberately, because you may well actually be hypnotizing yourself into your own stuckness. If only you stopped, you'd quickly see the other, much easier way.

I'm not joking about hypnotizing yourself to be fixated on an outcome. One definition of hypnosis is, 'a wakeful state of focused attention and heightened suggestibility, with diminished peripheral awareness'. To put it simply: tuning out all the other sources of information to focus on only one, usually the hypnotist's voice, but a voice is a voice, whether it's someone else's or the thoughts in your head. In fact, the thoughts in your head are far more powerful than any hypnotist's voice, but I guess you know that already, after all, you've been living with them, and their consequences.

If that voice, those thoughts, are repeating the same thing over and over and over again, you are literally hypnotizing yourself to stay stuck where you are. Not to mention the simple fact that when you are so intently focused on one thing, even if it seems like the right thing, you are missing everything else that's going on, perhaps missing the very opportunity you're so desperately looking for.

By holding so fixed an idea you are assuming, first, that it's the right idea, and secondly that it's the best outcome available. It may be the best you can *think* of, but that certainly doesn't mean it's the best possible.

FILLING IN THE GAPS

The problem with navigating only by what you know (by what's on your map) is that you know those things already. By definition you are filtering information only by what you already know is possible. And that doesn't seem very smart to me. I'd rather know what I know *and* have a way of extending my map and filling in some of the blanks, too. That's why you need to do it differently.

Navigating by logic alone is a bit like watching TV with the sound turned off. You're only getting part of the experience and missing out on lots of really cool stuff.

Actually, just to prove the point, next time you're watching the evening news, just turn the sound off and let your mind 'make up' what you think is going on. Then watch the later version with the sound on and notice how accurate you were, or not as the case may be…

It's time to tune in and turn up the volume, and let what's always been there guide you to better and easier decision-making.

This is how you find and keep on the right path. It'll be very easy once you know to trust it… once you know where you are going, your only – and I do mean *only* – goal should be to keep yourself in a good place every day so that you can notice and listen to your inner wisdom and then go with it.

LOOK AFTER YOURSELF

But that does mean you have to do something else differently. You're going to have to take care of yourself, every day. Before you run a mile, that doesn't mean you have to *do* anything; in fact, it might be an idea to do less and instead make some time for yourself and the things that nurture you every day – yes, every day! I've popped a few blank pages at the back of this book for you to use, so just take a minute now and note down what you can do, first of all once a month, to really nurture yourself. Then note down what you can do every week, and then what you can do every day. This can be the core foundation of your daily routine. Taking a little time to go to your foundation place will really make all the difference.

My own nurturing would be:

- Monthly – Read a good inspirational book (I read very slowly!)
- Weekly – Exercise, even if it's just a little bit, at least three times a week
- Daily – Get some fresh air and connect with nature, even if it is just sitting in my garden with a coffee, watching the birds.

When you get clear about what it is that you need to nurture yourself, these things become more than just 'nice to dos'. They become 'must dos' like brushing your teeth. I know I could get through the day without getting some fresh air, but I know I'll feel horrible and my heath will suffer if I neglect to nurture myself for too long.

As I said, you can pick things that take only a few minutes; it's amazing the difference just taking a little time to slow down and connect with whatever it is that energizes you will make.

As I've said before, this book has very little chance of having any effect on your life whatsoever unless you actually take action. This is one of those times. When you do make space and make the commitment to spend some time nurturing yourself every day, you will find the effortless energy which will propel you on your journey.

GETTING WHAT YOU WANT BY DOING WHAT YOU WANT – EASY!

It's the 'what you do' that matters, and of course you know by now that it doesn't have to be the hard-work-and-graft route (although that may well 'accelerate' the process for you), as I said earlier there has not yet been a system discovered where doing nothing equals getting lots. You have to get off your ass and do something; it might not have to be much, and is probably not what you're used to doing, but action is definitely required none the less.

More than Logic Alone

There is no doubt that you can get to where you want to be much more easily using more than logic alone. I suppose when I talk about setting the destination on your map (remember the symbol of the sports car or whatever represents success for you) I could also be talking about visualizing that which you want, or even attracting it into your life, but for me the process works at a deeper level. Remember, I am more interested in your powerful inner insights than your goals, the ones that give you your effortless energy.

So you set your course, but rather than looking to attract the end-result towards you, how about viewing it as looking for guidance to take you towards the objective? It's the difference between a 'fixed goal' and an inspiring idea or insight. That seems to be a better way to do it, as that way you are always moving forward, always on your journey and always open to new possibilities, and it frames things in a whole new way in your mind. Instead of the idea of sitting on the sofa and waiting for your goal to float magically through the door, surely it makes more sense to know it's out there and trust that something inside of you will help you to find it.

That just makes more sense to me. And, it suggests that you have to keep doing things in order to move forward in your life. Because as you move forward you are getting closer to your goal, all the while confidently reinforcing the idea that, because you are being guided by the compass of your inner knowing rather than just the logic of your outer map you can find, and then stay on, the right path for you.

In essence, this way puts all the control and knowing inside of you – and that's exactly where they should be. You have all you need to succeed right now. Perhaps you also have a few things that are stopping you, but as we've already discussed I'll bet those are more to do with thoughts and the meanings you give them than anything real or tangible.

Lining Up All the Parts

When you have all the parts lined up it can get very easy indeed – imagine getting what you want by doing what you want, wouldn't that be cool? You bet it is, and you can do exactly that starting right now. Even just thinking about it, I'll bet, gives you a sense of energy, doesn't it? I know it does for me; even just saying that phrase 'getting what I want by doing what I want' makes me feel better and more energized. I would encourage you to make that your daily mantra as you begin to go for it!

Oh, let me put another little health warning here: doing what you want does *not* mean being reckless with either yourself or others. Doing what you want means following your inner knowing or wanting. I may have wanted to stay in bed this morning, but that was just the little thought in my head complaining 'the alarm must be wrong and it can't possibly be time to get up yet, I've just closed my eyes...' You know the kind of thing. That was not what I *wanted* to do, it was just a thought; my real inner wanting was to get up and get on with things and enjoy the day. Caffeine always helps to shut up those early morning thoughts for me, as do music and fresh air, so I know all I have to do is put my feet on the floor, get to the kitchen, open the window, pop the kettle on and press the 'play' button on my iPod. By the time I've done that, the sleepy thoughts are gone and before I know it I'm into the day and looking forward to something I'm going to be doing.

A Quick Kick-start

Perhaps you'd like to find your own kick-start to the day. What are the three quick things you can do to get your day started off on the right track?

If I engaged with my negative morning thoughts, you can be sure I'd still be in bed doing what I 'thought' I wanted. It's a funny thing but it really is amazing the energy you can have and the amount you can do when you are in that place of going after what you want by doing what you want. But again, you do have to take action... and simple actions done consistently give big results.

IN ORDER TO GET, FIRST YOU HAVE TO GIVE

Getting back to making a difference, let me come back to my original point: what remarkable gift did you give to the world yesterday? What are you giving to the world today? If you're not doing it already, what are you going to give to the world today? If you want to receive something you have to give first, so what's it going to be?

Before you jump on that train of thought, just check in and make sure it's something you are happy to give and something that makes you feel good, too.

When the things you want to give are the things that help you get *and* make you feel good on the inside, you've got it cracked. Everything else will happen all by itself if you have the destination set and stay in that place where you know where you are going and know what it is that makes you feel good. You'll find a way, no problem at all.

The key here, though, is that to release the energy you have to be giving things you actually *want* to give. They're the things we have in abundance and that don't drain us. When we are giving what we don't really want to give, in order to get something in return, then it all goes a bit wrong. But when you sit in the place of giving what you want to give and receiving what you want to receive, then you have found the perfect balance.

A CARING KICK – IN THE RIGHT DIRECTION

For the next 24 hours I'd love for you to get very clear about saying 'No' when you need to. Not 'Maybe' or 'I might,' those are just soft 'No's, and the problem with them is that as soon as you have said them you feel two extra pressures: you know you really wanted to say 'No' and so you're now wondering how you can actually say that and what your excuse will be, and of course you are also feeling the pressure of knowing that the time is looming when you'll have to give a definite answer and let someone (who has now got their hopes up) down. Get used to saying 'No' when you mean no, and also setting some boundaries around what you are truly happy to give when you say 'Yes.'

What Are Your No-brainer Yeses?

It all comes down to knowing what your powerful personal insights are. Getting clear on what you have to give makes a valuable difference in achieving your goals, and helps you to steer a path with the compass of your intuition to keep you in that place where effort is effortless and success becomes easy.

If you've not done so yet, this is definitely the place to put your thinking cap on and maybe even put the book down for a bit and really check in with your intuition. Allow yourself to get clear on what you really want. The quieter you get, the more you will notice your insights and inspiring ideas. Not the stuff on the outside, but the feelings they represent? The feeling of security and abundance and your ability to create might be represented by £1,000,000 in the bank or a sports car, but it's not the *source* of the feelings or the energy.

What Is Your True Energy Source?

Please don't continue until you are clear on this. The rest of the book all follows on from the premise that you at least have an idea of where you're going, and that it's a direction shaped from the inside-out and inspired by insights. In other words, it's what your inner knowing knows you want.

Once you're ready and know what your powerful inner goal is – and remember, it's not necessarily the manifestation of a specific thing like 'I want to be a surgeon' or 'I want to drive a luxury sports car,' but rather the underlying 'I want to make a difference,' 'I want to be abundant,' 'I want to feel good in myself,' etc. – the next question is: 'What are you going to give joyfully as the first step towards your goal?'

Again, this is the time to connect with your inner knowing. I hope you've been playing with this already, but don't worry, I'm not talking about some deep meditative state (although that may work if you enjoy that kind of thing). I'm talking about spending some time with the real you. It might be that you sit and close your eyes and go inside and ask your subconscious for the answer, or it might be that you set a question in your mind: 'What's the right thing for me to give to move forward right now?' Then go for a walk or sit in the garden and listen to the birds, or do any of the other things that you know make you feel the most 'you'. I know that if I'm struggling for an answer I usually just set the question in my mind and then go and do something fun, something that puts me firmly in 'flow' – after all, that's when I'm at my most intelligent and not restricted by the boundaries of my logical map.

IQ and EQ

There is a big difference between logical intelligence (IQ) and emotional intelligence or knowing (EQ).

Remember, IQ logic gets you through school, but emotional intelligence (EQ) gets you through life. The textbook definition of one's emotional quotient (EQ) is 'a measure of your ability to notice and then manage your interior and exterior perceptions of your feelings and then control your reactions.' We'll just call it navigating around your map using your inner compass. Your mood will always control your ability to resolve any situation. If you're feeling bad you must be having 'bad' thoughts. Don't try to think your way through it; do something to make yourself feel better instead. Simple!

So what does your emotionally intelligent inner compass tell you to do to find the answer?

A CARING KICK – IN THE RIGHT DIRECTION

Find what's right for you, there is no wrong here. The goal is to get to the place where you know what you want (the powerful underlying energizing goals, remember) and you also know the first step to take, the first bit of energy you can give to begin the process and then, of course, take action!

What's the first thing you can do joyfully today?

I suppose it actually comes down to what we could call the three Cs of success: clarity, choice and creativity.

Clarity

The first, I'm hoping, is fairly self-explanatory. You obviously need to have clarity to know what you want and the awareness of knowing what to do in order to start the journey towards that.

Maybe your journey doesn't even need to begin with a clear insight of 'Right, I'm going to do *that*.' Maybe the better way is just to get clear on some things that you might like to 'try out', some ideas you might like to explore before you commit to which one you're going to go with.

Even by doing that you are committing to the most important thing of all: you are committing to take action of some kind and committing to allowing yourself to move forward with clarity. Once you've taken the brake off you're on your way, the only bit still to be found is propulsion, but that will come easily with the energy of knowing you are following your path and steering the course very much from within and NOT from the crappy thoughts that might pop up from time to time. Remember those thoughts are just thoughts, you do not have to do anything with them. Just like they could keep me in bed in the morning, they can keep you stuck if you let them. What's your new kick-start routine again?

Thoughts only have the power you give them, and when you give the thoughts no power you give them no point. It's as simple as that.

When you make the thoughts powerless you also make them pointless.

Your mind has a wonderful ability to create, but just as you can create solutions so you can create problems. Having the awareness that thoughts are just thoughts, having the consciousness to notice them and then of course the ability to let them go and be free to make your own choice, is very powerful.

Choice

When you have broken the habit of engaging with your thoughts, you set yourself free to make the choices you want to make instead of being pulled out of shape by the habit of engaging with your thoughts and then reacting to the meanings you make up.

You have the choice to 'do' and 'be' exactly as you want to be.

I am a firm believer that freedom and choice are the two most powerful and empowering things that we can enjoy, and if I can help you to experience them in your life I'll be delighted, because from that point you can create whatever you want for yourself.

Creativity

When you strip everything else way, all the 'shoulds' and 'logic' and thoughts, you are left with a blank sheet of paper on which to create whatever you want.

It doesn't really matter where you are starting from, it's where you're going that counts, and you can change anything you want right now. As soon as you realize that, you can enjoy creating wonderful possibilities in your life.

I was working with a client the other day, she was stuck in a rut, had been to university and studied a 'good' subject, one that her parents were proud of, and shed got a 'good' job in the corporate world, but with each day that passed and every time she went to the big shiny office in the city she felt that the life she should really have was passing her by, like she had taken a wrong turning somewhere many years before and was paying the price daily.

She was only in her early thirties but felt like she had messed up her life in a way that no one in her family could understand. She had outperformed everyone she knew and was very successful, but totally unfulfilled.

It turned out she really wanted to be a doctor, that was her true calling and she longed to be of 'service'. 'So what stops you?' I asked. 'Well, my grades weren't quite good enough at school, I could have gone back and done another year to improve them but I guess I thought I might as well take the other place open to me and do that, it's not like it's a bad job.'

'Ah, thought justifying the previous thought,' I thought. Are you still with me? Good…

'But that wasn't my question. My question was, "What stops you?" Not "what stopped you?"'

'Oh, no, I couldn't do it now. I'm way too old, and besides how do I know I'm up to it anyway?'

'Too old, hmmm… it takes about seven years to qualify as a doctor, right? So by my reckoning you would be 40.'

'Erm, yes, and…'

'And you'd still have a good 25 years of doing what you love before you'd be of age to retire… sounds great to me… So, what *really* stops you?'

As I'm sure you can imagine, we played with this back and forth for quite a while before she concluded that actually the only thing stopping her were the stories she told herself about why she couldn't or shouldn't do it… I know I would definitely prefer 25 years of doing something I loved rather than 30-odd years doing something that makes me miserable every day. When you put it like that it sounds obvious, but for most of us, as with my client, the inertia to break free from the stuckness and the fear was really strong. But it was only really ever stories keeping her stuck anyway.

She was very clear on what she wanted to do, no doubt about that. Every part of her wanted to be a doctor. The only thing holding her stuck was the stories she was telling herself about why she couldn't. Do you want to know the really cool part? As soon as she began to consider the idea seriously, as soon as she took the brake off, her creative mind kicked in and she started to think of all the ways she 'could' do it…

One of her big fears was how she could support herself while she studied, but she had now committed to taking the action to stop dismissing the possibility and just explore what the options there might be.

You can't imagine the smile on my face when a few days later the phone rang and she told me that 'just by chance' she had bumped into someone she used to work with and they told her their company was looking for someone like her to work part-time, or in fact, even better still, would be someone working on a contract working one day a week.

Contract work always pays better because of the risk and lack of staff benefits, but that was fine with her; she'd much rather the cash than the healthcare at that point, hopefully there would be plenty of that where she was going... The contract would enable her to work one day a week for the equivalent of two and a half days' pay – not a fortune but enough to pay her way and have loads of time to study. She even figured that if she applied her corporate work ethic to her studies she could make that day up easily. Brilliant! I know who I'd want to have by my bedside if I ever need it...

This is perhaps where my approach and the law of attraction come back together: did she 'attract' the opportunity into her life? Well, I think she probably did, *but* she did so by taking action not just by going home and wishing things would change. She gave energy to the situation and created some space free from the limiting beliefs of her thoughts, and allowed herself to enjoy the synchronicity of that state of flow...

Wherever you are right now you have the ability to create the change you want, and it can be easier that you think. The funny thing is that you tend to get more of whatever it is you're focusing on. If you're focused on being stuck, you'll likely get more stuck, but if you're focusing on opportunities, guess what? You'll get more of those, too…

As I have explained in an earlier chapter, you don't have to know all the steps you're going to take, all the events you're going to enjoy and 'coincidences' you're going to come across along the way. The difference between success and failure is in the way you approach them and the way you use, and harness, what's on the inside to affect the world on the outside…

As I'll show you in the next chapter, in order for this to happen you first have to get clear of the crappy limiting thoughts, and stay in a place where you can notice the opportunities that come your way and take action when they find you.

You do need to be clear on what it is you really want and where you are heading, but as I've said before you don't need to know how you're going to get there yet. In fact you may never know all the steps, maybe never more than one or two steps ahead, but that's all part of the fun.

WHAT WILL MAKE YOU COME ALIVE?

What is it that, when you think about it being an effortless part of your life, just gives you a wonderful, energized feeling? If you've not got this clear yet, then please, please do that now. Let me repeat: you do not need to know how you are going to get there, just where 'there' is… or, to be totally correct, what you'll find there, what is it that you will be doing or having or feeling when you are 'there', when you have it. That's your goal, and a worthy destination, one that your subconscious will have no problem propelling you towards.

Plot your point on the map now and then just relax (this is the easy way to success, remember). That's all you need to do, and here's a little space to do it in. Just note down right here what it is that you want, but remember it's about what you'll enjoy when you get there. I'm not saying the journey will be easy, but the method is simple – and if the goal is real and true to you then you'll have no problem, and will even come to enjoy the challenges along the way.

I remember when one of my clients was complaining some years ago about something feeling like an uphill struggle, I said to them, 'Mountain climbing would be no fun if there was no mountain,' and while at the time I'm sure he had no idea what I was on about, and probably thought I was mad, he did tell me years later that it now made total sense and that he'd come to enjoy the challenges just as much as the success. The difference is in the story he told himself about it. They were all part of his journey on his path, and he learned more from those times than from the time spent free-wheeling down the other side of the mountain - although the freewheeling was definitely more fun!

CHAPTER 9

OPPORTUNITY IN ACTION

One of the things that has been most fun and also most enlightening for me from my own journey so far has been that I've been able to develop my awareness and an understanding of what I had actually been doing completely naturally but had just never noticed.

In this chapter I'm going to share with you the simplest and most effective model I know to get the best from your life. But before I do that, I'd like to share a story with you by way of illustration, to show you that you don't have to have it all figured out, ever... It's the story of one of my own journeys through personal development and also to my biggest payday to date.

Do you remember I said that you don't need to know all the steps you'll take when you start out? In fact that's not even possible, so please stop trying to figure them all out. All you have to do is know where you're heading and what's the next step.

What do Rosie the tarantula, whom you met earlier, a granny, a TV 'Gladiator', a Navy pilot, a Middle Eastern diplomat and a marketing guru all have in common? No, they're not the line-up of a new reality TV show. What they all have in common is *me*. Let me explain…

MINIS TO FERRARIS

Some years ago I had been lucky enough to have a piece in one of the tabloids about me helping someone get over their spider phobia. Very kindly the journalist gave me the opportunity to expand my private practice by putting my phone number at the end of the article, so as you might expect I got a lot of calls from people all over the country with all manner of fears and phobias, some I'd never even heard of at that point. But one stands out now above all others, and although I didn't realize it at the time would be the one that would change my life, for now.

It was a call from a woman named Trish, living in a small town about an hour's drive from me. She was a granny and had recently had a near-miss when a road accident happened right beside her when she was driving home one day. Although nothing had actually happened to her, she'd understandably got a hell of a shock as a van hit a bus just a few feet away from her. So she'd parked up and taken a taxi home.

That was the last time she'd driven. Every time she got in the car her mind flashed back to that day and she just couldn't do it. Her husband had tried everything he could think of, he'd even bought her a new car, a beautiful brand new Mini Cooper soft top.

When I met Trish, 'Millie', her Mini, had just a few miles on the clock and her grandson had been in it more often than she had. Anyway, to cut a long story short I went to see her and cured her driving phobia, and of course to prove she was cured and to give her a little extra confidence we went for a drive, right past the scene of the accident... she was fine!

We were both delighted and I was feeling quite good about myself as I drove back home that day. I was only jolted from my thoughts (I was driving carefully, honest officer) by my phone ringing. It was a journalist from a rival newspaper to the one the initial story about my work had been in. They had seen the spider piece and wondered if I might have any other stories they could run - the only catch was that it had to be something 'very visual', something that would look good in the newspaper. My mind was blank, I'd helped people with fears of needles, dogs, lots more spiders, storms, bananas or anything that looked like a banana (yes, really) and obviously Trish, just nothing you'd call very visual, but as I drove and because it was a lovely sunny day I decided to take the scenic route, out into the countryside and past Knockhill Racing Circuit with all its high-octane advertising hoardings. I don't know why the 'Ferrari experience' stood out from all the rest, maybe because I'm a bit of a car fan, I'm not sure, but my little brain started whirring into action. 'Wait a minute, Trish in her Mini might not be very visual, but Trish is a grandmother. A granny in a Ferrari! Now that's visual...'

I did three things very quickly. I called the racetrack and asked, 'If I could get you coverage in the national media could

I have the use of your Ferrari for an hour?' 'For nothing!'
Done, then I called Trish. 'How do you fancy driving a Ferrari
round a racetrack?' Done… and then I called the journalist
back 'Would a granny in a Ferrari work for you?' 'How's
Tuesday?' Done… Perfect!

Now, you might think that was opportunism in the extreme,
but the way I saw it, if Trish could drive a Ferrari round a
racetrack with me beside her, then her Mini would be no
problem. The racetrack got some free publicity, as of course
did I, and the newspaper got a great feature… we'd all win.

'Granny Gets Racy!' turned out to be a really great piece.

But that wasn't the end of it. Another opportunity was just
about to pop up. On the day we went to drive the Ferrari,
the PR people at the circuit had also arranged for a group
of women journalists to come and experience the thrills of
motorsport. As we all enjoyed a much-needed coffee to
keep out the cold, we got chatting, and while they all loved
the story of Trish in the Ferrari, one journalist in particular
jumped at the idea of doing a piece on life coaching. In fact,
she had been in the original series of the TV show *Gladiators*
but was now a columnist for one of the broadsheets. We
popped a date in the diary for me to help her with some of
her personal stuff, tuning up her sports performance. The
session worked a treat and the resulting feature appeared in
print on New Year's Day. Another great opportunity and a
great result!

There is just no way I could have made this series of events happen – but it gets better. All I had to do was stay in the flow, spot the opportunities and take action when they arose, but another piece of the puzzle was just about to slot into place.

FLYING HIGH

There was a guy sitting at home that New Year's Day gently working off his over-indulgence of the night before in the comfort of an armchair, reading the newspaper. He'd just left the navy, where he had been a pilot, and was in the process of setting up his own air charter business. But he was having some doubts. 'Perhaps I should get a proper job instead?' he was thinking. He was still wrestling with his dilemma when he turned to the back of the paper, and there under the headline 'Head Master' he read about a life coach who'd been helping people to achieve the lives they wanted to live (er, me). 'Perhaps I should give him a call?' he thought, and a few days later that's exactly what he did…

Kev would become a great client, and he did indeed start that air charter business, shuttling the rich and famous around in his own private helicopter.

Actually Kev would become a good friend, too, and would be the next pivotal piece in the jigsaw for me, even though I still didn't know it… You see, one of the 'homework' exercises I'd given him (a bit like your 'caring kicks') was to research and attend some courses… The piece of his puzzle that was missing was 'information', and as you know already, if it's just information and 'how to' you're lacking, then you're not really stuck. Fortunately it wasn't anything to do with the actual flying (thankfully), but how to promote and market his business. I guess there's not much call for that in the Navy. You turn up, the helicopter's ready, someone tells you where to point it and off you go.

So Kev set about finding the missing piece that was keeping him stuck by attending some courses on sales and marketing, which of course, being someone who wanted to ensure his success, he duly did.

One of my biggest learnings in my early days working for myself was that you don't have to know everything and don't have to do everything yourself. You can take a big shortcut and save yourself a lot of pain (and often money) in the long run by finding someone who already knows the way and getting them to guide you, or even better by just asking them to do that bit for you.

I remember coaching a client who needed a website for his business. Not wanting to spend anymore than he had to, he went to the library and got a book on web design and sat down to begin learning… not a bad plan, you might be thinking. But when his income was dependant on him getting his message out to the world, then every day that he didn't have a site up was costing him potential bookings… So was it really such a smart move to spend weeks learning how to build a site, never mind actually building one? I'm thinking not, though I do understand the logic behind it. I'm just not sure what made him think that his first attempt at a home-made website would be as good or better than he could have had in a fraction of the time from a professional. And he could have used the time saved to generate more sales, or even to get better at what he does, which is not building websites… Do you see my point?

Anyway, Kev wasn't like that, and when faced with the challenge of how to learn to market his business he decided to go right to the top and invest in a course being run by someone who'd made millions out of marketing other people's products and who is one of the best in the business. It turned out to be a smart move for me, too, although I didn't even know it at the time.

I, too, was looking to make some changes in my business and wanted to expand away from my coaching and therapy practice and develop a more secure 'multi-channel' income model. I had hatched a plan to diversify into products that could help more people (maybe even write a book)… if only I knew how. I need not have worried, because I was in flow and the next opportunity was just about to present itself, and right when I needed it.

Part of the deal Kev had done for his marketing course was that he got to attend the next workshop his new marketing guru was running and he could bring a friend 'free of charge'… even better, and as a Scotsman that was music to my ears. All it would cost me was my flight. So yes, you've guessed it, off I went…

STAYING OPEN

I really had no idea what to expect as I arrived at the conference venue, save to say that I had a bit of a feeling that something good would come of it. I often get that feeling and know it so well now I just don't question it anymore. I don't need to know the purpose of a meeting or a trip, if I have that feeling I'm there, no question!

That feeling is my intuition, my inner knowing, and is very much the compass by which I navigate. If I have the feeling, count me in! No feeling, hmmm, not so sure I want to be doing it.

But that morning I did have the feeling, and so although I had no idea what would come of it I took my seat and was ready to learn. The day was very interesting indeed, but somehow I knew that the teaching being delivered wasn't really for me. Yes, of course I learned a lot, but I just couldn't see myself putting the strategies into action. The route just didn't seem right. I could see that if I did use the principles they would work, but it just didn't feel like the right path for me. I felt really disappointed. How could this be? I'd been so certain, but maybe I'd been wrong. I started to doubt what I thought I knew. It's easy done…

But because I know better than that, at the final coffee break of the day I asked myself how something that felt right could now feel wrong? And then I shut up…

THE MAGIC IN THE MIX

Then it occurred to me: the right path was not in learning and then going and doing it for myself, the real magic was in the mix. Somewhere in the combination of Kev, myself and the marketing guru (Tim), lay the answer. 'Got it!' I thought. Now all I had to do was to make that happen. Remember, at this point I had no idea *what* would happen, but my intent really was strong. I was going to diversify my business and I was fully in tune with my inner knowing. Now all I had to do was convince a very successful and busy multi-millionaire that his next big project should be me! Even although I didn't actually know what my 'product' was yet, I just knew that if I could build one and get him to market it, we'd be on to a winner!

I waited until the end of the day and approached Tim, thanked him for the course and the opportunity to attend (for free), and then made my move: 'How would you feel about a joint venture? If I put a product together and you market it, we could be on to something.' Now, you have to remember that we had never met each other before and so it was perhaps a little premature of me to mention this, but we did resolve to explore whether there was something we could do together. I guess we both kind of knew there was something in it even if neither of us knew exactly what at the time. (I've since learned that Tim navigates by his gut feeling every bit as much as I do.)

We did indeed keep in touch and even had a couple of meetings, and after each one I kept thinking up possibilities of what we could do and how cool the weight loss product we were now discussing could be – but still it wasn't quite right; for me it all felt a little, well, logical, and I guess for Tim it must have felt like just another meeting in his already very busy schedule of projects. It wasn't until a throwaway remark at the end of one such meeting that I really knew it would go somewhere.

ANOTHER NEW YEAR'S DAY

Tim was going to spend New Year in Dubai with his family. What a *coincidence*, I was scheduled also to be in Dubai from the 3rd of January. Quickly and instinctively I made a decision: I would go to Dubai a few days earlier and tag on a short holiday at the start of the trip. That would be nice and it would give Tim and me the opportunity to meet up. Which is exactly what we did. Over lunch in the sunshine of Dubai, the foundations of what would become 'The Slim Girl's Box of Secrets' would be laid.

This, my first product, was launched a year later and, to my delight, is helping women in 52 countries (at the last count) to lose weight easily. It's also given me by far my biggest payday to date… Tim and I are now good friends and the project has grown in scope beyond our wildest dreams, and I'm sure the resultant spin-offs will make many dreams come true for us and lots of others, too.

NO LOGIC REQUIRED

But the best bit of this journey from my driving phobic granny to the launch of an international product is that there has been very little logic involved. There is no way I could possibly have planned any of it, no way I could have made it happen if I'd tried. On the balance of logic and probability, the odds of it all happening would be unbelievably small, and yet it did and these things continue to happen every day. It's the same way I met my wife, the same way my own path changed direction and the same way I have learned is without doubt the right and indeed only way – to live from my inner knowing and it's not in my head.

Maybe you think you don't know best? Well, not logically anyway…

For me the real path of success is intuition, opportunity and action. Those three parts in harmony are the key to living in and from the space I want to live from and the way that my life – and yours – can be easy.

I have always had the belief that if it feels easy it's probably right, and if it feels hard it's probably not. Now I know why that's true. Please don't get me wrong, that is not to say that success doesn't require hard work – of course it does. But when you've got the balance right it often feels like someone or something is giving you a helping hand. An invisible and intangible force is helping you towards your goals, and the work itself doesn't feel so hard because you actually *want* to do it; it's an effortless effort.

I know this might be sounding a little weird to the logical part of your brain, but in my experience success comes much more from getting into, and then staying in, the space where good things happen than it does from graft and sweat and hard work. So how do you find your flow and then keep yourself in that space?

A CARING KICK – IN THE RIGHT DIRECTION

Let's go back to a previous exercise. You'll remember I asked you to spend some time just navigating by your gut feeling, yes? Just going with what you feel even if you don't immediately know why? Right, well, it's time to take that one stage further.

When I get one of 'those' feelings, I know that my own well-being is guiding me. I always ask myself 'What might it mean?' or 'What opportunity could be here for me, what am I being made aware of?' That's the navigating by your intuition and noticing part, and of course you'll want to check that against your map of the world, too.

Next is the opportunity. These two parts (intuition and opportunity) are very closely linked, and at first you will have to be quite self-aware to spot them.

The trick, of course, comes from allowing that small voice within to speak to you so that you are navigating by your sense of knowing and not by the clatter of other thoughts. The difference – and you'll recognize it quickly when you get to know it better – is to listen to what you are being told and not to what you are making up. I know this might sound a bit weird and an odd concept, but once you tune in to it you will know exactly what I mean.

Have you ever walked into a room and found someone you know well speaking on the phone to someone else you know well? You can tell who they are on the phone to even though you can only hear muffled sounds from the phone. Why? Because you are so familiar with the voice and the speech patterns of the other person that you can clearly identify them from very little information.

It's a lot like this when you learn to notice your inner knowing. You might not necessarily know what it's saying exactly, but you should know it's there and then stop to listen. My experience is that it is almost never wrong.

Once you've noticed, you've listened and spotted the opportunity, then it's time to take action! It must be full steam ahead for success central then, is it?

Ah, well, not quite so fast. You see, if you do that you're almost bound to close yourself off to the next bit of guidance. The route to your success is seldom a straight line. You will have to make many adjustments and corrections along the way – and how do you know what they are and when to make them? Well, you listen to your intuition, and then to the small voice of opportunity, and then you take action – and then you keep repeating this process over and over again.

FLYING THROUGH LIFE

Let me put it like this: I want you to imagine that you have to pilot an aircraft from one place to another. Now, I don't know if you have ever flown a plane, but in essence it goes a bit like this: turn the engines on, let the thrust they produce propel you forward, point at the sky and then steer and correct your course until you get to where you're heading. OK, OK, I know it's a lot more complicated than that, but basically it boils down to those steps.

This idea was first brought home to me when I took a flight in a very small plane over the Scottish Highlands; it was treat, and whereas on the big commercial planes all I would usually think about was which movie was next, this was very different.

As we flew low over the Highlands, our little plane being buffeted by the wind and thermal air currents, I couldn't help but wonder if this was what some people felt like in their lives… continually being blown off-course and fighting to make any progress in the right direction.

The scenery was in stark contrast to that at the beginning of the flight. We had taken off from Cumbernauld, once voted the 'most dismal place in Scotland' (although I believe they are working on changing that), and yet I was soon looking down on the majestic, rugged beauty of the Highlands. I guess where you start from is not so important – the journey through life is yours to explore.

I know the Highlands well and delighted in picking out some of my favourite landmarks, and this time I could see all the highlights at once, like playing join-the-dots with the Scottish landscape. I guess you could say that I could see the bigger picture, and boy did it look different. Suddenly, from 8,000 feet, great mountains looked small and I could see things from a new perspective. I was also able to put so many things into the correct proportion in other areas of my life.

The only thing disturbing me was the pilot's constant fidgeting right beside me. From the moment we took off he had been moving levers, adjusting switches and checking his instruments. Was this normal? Apparently it was. A plane never flies in a straight line from A to B. Not even the big ones you get on as you head off to the sun. Instead the pilot (or auto-pilot) is constantly making adjustments, correcting the flight path to account for wind and weather, other aircraft and many other unforeseen factors to fly the easiest – but not always the shortest – route and ensure that you touch down safely.

It struck me that this really is the same in life, but how often have you set your flight plan thinking you know where you're heading and then allowed yourself to be blown off-course at the first gust of unexpected wind? Or tried so hard to take the direct route that it has turned out this very single-mindedness has been your undoing?

The key to reaching your goals is first of all to know what they are. Set your flight plan – but then have enough flexibility in your approach to make any adjustments you need to. There are numerous ways to get where you want to go, and the problem with focus is that, by definition, you are excluding a whole lot of other routes. Keep your eye on the destination, but not on your preconceived ideas of how you might get there.

Right, now let me bring it back to you and navigating through your life from now on.

You have your engines of effortless effort for propulsion, because you are following the path you want to follow and that's right for you – though just as an aside I have found that motivation is always directly in proportion to how much you really want to get to your destination. If you find yourself lacking in motivation, maybe it's not your engines that need attention; maybe you're pointing them somewhere you don't really want to go or somewhere that your intuition knows isn't right for you?.

Just a thought, but definitely worth thinking about. You'll find that when you have the right goal, the one that you really want and that all parts of you want, then motivation will not be a problem.

Anyway, we'll assume you have your desire and motivation sorted. So, destination, check! Engines of desire on and running at full speed, check! What next?

I don't know. Why don't you ask, on the inside? The compass you are going to use on this journey is within you, the compass you are going to use on your journey is your compass of intuition and inner knowing, set beside your map of learning. When you bring together what you know and what you've learned, you have all the information you'll ever need.

But, just like a plane flying from A to B, the path you are taking may be a straight line briefly but never for very long. As the pilot of your flight through life you will have to make lots and lots of adjustments for all sorts of unforeseen events and also lots of other opportunities along the way.

The way I like to do it is first of all to get very clear on my destination, insight or inspiring idea, and then set my next action by where I feel my energy and enthusiasm are, where I feel my motivation wants to take me on the first part of the journey. I say 'the first part', because that's all you have to know. All you need to know is where you are now and what the next step to take is. What's the next step you feel you want to take?

Lots of people stop short of even trying for their dreams because they can't see or figure out all the steps they need to take, and so they don't take even that first one. I know that logically it makes sense to know where you're going and how you are going to get there, but in a very different way that rigid focus can be exactly the thing that stops you from ever leaving the ground.

Let me take you through the process step by step.

A CARING KICK – IN THE RIGHT DIRECTION

1   Identify the inspiring ideas that make you come alive. If you haven't already then now would be a good time to make a list...

2   Ask yourself: 'If I didn't know any better, what would I do first?' Please go ahead and do that now, and then just notice what comes up for you. I'll bet it won't be a 'logical' answer, but I'll double bet it'll be a powerful one.

3   Whatever comes up for you, the only thing you have to do now is to take action... it doesn't have to be a big deal, although I know it can feel a bit scary at first when you are doing something that you cannot logically explain. Just think of it as an exploration, and look forward to what you might discover.

4   Do whatever you need to do to nurture yourself and stay in your own personal flow every day.

If you go into this with a logical and preconceived idea of the outcome, you will be falling into the old trap of listening to your thoughts and giving them meaning. We know that doing that can only lead you to a place where you are disappointed and frustrated.

Take action with the sole purpose and intention of 'finding out': finding out what it means and finding out what other opportunity might be down the path, if only you take the first step.

The way I like to do it is to keep my intention on my inspiration and desired outcome but keep my focus on the day-to-day, and specifically on keeping myself in the space where good things happen and I can notice opportunities when they show up.

Set your destination and rev up your motivation engines by making sure it's something you really do want. Then keep your daily focus on doing whatever you need to do in that day to stay in the space where good things happen seemingly all by themselves and you can notice them when they do.

JUST GETTING ON WITH IT

That's the secret to just getting on with it: when the energy of the engines of motivation are carrying you forward to somewhere that you actually want to go, you are giving what you want to give. All you need to do is just stay in the 'authentic me' space where that can happen, and happen easily.

You may already have experience of this happening, although perhaps not consciously. Often it happens just after we give up and stop trying. Most people have had an experience of this, like at a job interview – you know the kind of thing, and I'm sure you, like most people, have experienced something like this. 'I need to come across as natural and confident, but wait, not *too* natural or *too* confident, I don't want them to think I'm cocky. OK, so I need to assume the role and act like the person they want to hire. OK, so I need to be myself and also be completely fake at the same time… argh!' And of course you get through it, but I'll bet when you leave the building you suddenly have an enlightened moment when the perfect answer to the killer question just pops into your head. 'If only I'd said that instead, why didn't I think of it? Well, I'll never get the job now, that answer would have been so much better…' and then you probably spend the rest of the day beating yourself up about all the other wonderfully witty and intelligent things you could have said if only you'd thought of them at the time.

Do you think it's a coincidence that when you *stop* worrying about what you 'should' do or say you suddenly get a lot smarter? I think not! Wouldn't it just be a better idea to live from that 'authentic you' place all the time? That's when you're at your best, that's when you're most intelligent and that's when it can all be much easier.

It's a funny thing, but when you're in this space it is as if something bigger than you or something outside of you is conspiring to help, and in ways that you could not have imagined. What if that bigger thing is not on the outside but right there on the inside, and it's there in you right now? I think we have all experienced periods in our lives when things just go really well, when things click into place for no apparent reason and we find ourselves very quickly where we wanted to be.

FOLLOWING THE *RIGHT* PATH

For those brief periods – and for most of us those are places we pass through rather than live day to day – you were living on the path that was right for you and navigating by what you knew was right, and then allowing it to just flow. Of course, what normally happens then is that you begin to listen to the thoughts and doubts in your head and go back to navigating by logic, and you stop paying attention to your inner knowing.

Even if this is with the best of intentions, if you run off down the path but then stop listening to your intuition, you might go too far and get just as lost as if you'd never started. Then of course your logical head has even more ammunition: 'Ah this intuition thing's not to be trusted, look where it got us.' So when you first start navigating by intuition and inner knowing, please do not get scared, do not doubt it, just enjoy the exploration and enjoy the ride. And, as I've said a few times now, start with the small stuff until you get the hang of it.

It's a bit like steering a bike down a twisty hill, the forward motion is effortless and staying on the right track might take a bit of exertion and be a bit wobbly at first, but when you get it right and you're in that state of flow, your journey can be easier and more fun than you could ever imagine. And all because you allow it to be. This is not something you can force, this is something you must allow to happen.

Allow yourself to detach from the thoughts in your head. They only have the power you give them, they are not true; they are not a documentary, they are a story.

Allow yourself to notice your inner knowing and the strength of your intuition.

Allow yourself to trust that knowing, and then allow yourself to take the effortless action you want to… for just as long as you know is right for you, while always navigating with your map of learning and your compass of knowing. You can be wherever you are meant to be faster than you could ever have imagined and with less stress and more fun, too… now doesn't that sound like something you'd love to do?

I bet it does! Well, there's nothing stopping you. *Just get on with it.*

CHAPTER 10

SHY KIDS GET NO CHOCOLATE

As we approach the end of this book I'm hoping that you are already incorporating some of my suggestions into your daily life? If you are, then I'm sure you'll be noticing some differences already.

As I've said before, small changes really can make a very big difference. If you are already on your way, then congratulations. But if not, why not? What's going on?

Are you waiting until the end of the book before you start?

Maybe you're waiting for the perfect conditions, for everything to be lined up perfectly?

We have a saying in Scotland (mainly amongst hill walkers): 'If you're waiting for the perfect weather you'll never leave the house.' The path will never be without rocks, and the sky (or schedule) never completely clear – but that doesn't mean you can't have a great day and enjoy the freedom, and of course the view…

Maybe you're just not quite sure about it all yet?

Maybe there's a little voice saying something like, 'Well, this is all very interesting but I'm not sure it'll work for me.' If there is, that's totally cool; I was exactly the same. But if you don't do anything new you're certainly not going to find out. Why not think of this journey as an exploration to find out whatever there is to find, instead of a definitive and slightly daunting life changing experience? The former certainly sounds much easier and more fun to me.

You already know that the change you seek doesn't have to be difficult, but you do have to go for it, you do have to commit to making a difference, first 'in' your life and then 'with' your life.

I love the phrase, 'Shy kids get no chocolate.' I first heard it many years ago from a mature and experienced businesswoman during a meeting. I was new to the company and a little shy at the time, and was procrastinating over something, not sure what to do, when she said, 'Speak up, son. Shy kids get no chocolate.' In other words, stand up for yourself, challenge things, take control and don't just let life happen to you.

Just get on with it, because if you don't you definitely won't get anything new (well, probably not anything you'd actually want).

There is no method yet invented where doing nothing equals getting lots. Sure, the old idea of doing lots in order to get lots has been soundly disproven, too, but you do still need to do *something*, the right thing, and the right thing for you.

As you know already, it's not the things on the outside that are stopping you or keeping you stuck; it's your thoughts on the inside *about* the things on the outside.

You have very little direct control on the physical world, but you do have complete control on what happens inside of you: your reaction to your thoughts, the meanings you give them, the feelings they generate and the actions you take – in those steps something that doesn't exist (thoughts) can shape your existence (actions).

LET'S BRING ALL THE THREADS TOGETHER

Oh, if you're one of those people who skips from the first to the last chapter, this will be useful but not nearly as useful as if you'd read all the pages in between.

- The imagined turns into reality – whether you like it or not.
- The 'just get on with it' approach really is inside-out and, if I may remind you, the process goes something like this:
  1. You have a thought (which we know you have no control over) and which you either engage with it or you don't.
  2. If you engage with the thought, you then have

to give it meaning and that meaning 'could' be true, but the vast majority of the time it isn't definitely true. *But*, because the thought in your head sounds just like you and you think you'd never lie to yourself, you tend to believe it without question, and then automatically feel the feelings that go with that thought and belief. Once you're feeling the feelings the actions are inevitable...

- While most interventions focus on things you can do to make everything OK once you are feeling bad, I would prefer if you just didn't feel bad in the first place. It just seems easier that way.

- When you think about it like that, it makes sense not to get carried away and automatically engage with your thoughts, since, contrary to popular belief, they are not always right. Next time you find yourself engaging with one of those random thoughts in your head, just stop. Don't be shy, challenge it: 'Is this thought really true or have I just made it up?'

- The way to change your physical life is to change your virtual life – the thoughts on the inside that, if left unchecked, can become very real. But of course they don't start of that way; they are just thoughts until you act otherwise.

- The precursor to all action is always thought. Intangible thoughts can result in very real things happening but in the beginning thoughts are just thoughts, generated by your mind. You can be aware of them through the power of your consciousness,

but in reality they are just make-believe until you make them otherwise.

Do you remember my client who was longing to be a doctor but was stuck in a rut and miserable? What was it that kept her in the grave with the ends knocked out? It wasn't really her missed opportunity or the lack of options; it was her thoughts about those things. Or the woman with the 'gay' boyfriend who ran out of the bar in disgust and didn't slept for the next two weeks, over nothing that was real even though it certainly felt very real to her. All caused by thoughts, all just made up.

And then, of course, there's you. You picked up this book for a reason, to find the answer, to find the missing secrets or widget or pearl of wisdom that would make everything OK, that magic 'thing' which, once you had it, would make you a success... and that too is just a thought that is keeping you stuck. 'When I have that thing that I've not got yet, then I can be successful, but not before.' I'll bet this is not the first time you've looked for it, either? Can you see how that train of thought, even though you were seeking the source of your success, was encouraging you to look in the wrong places?

The source of your success is on the inside and always has been.

Those thoughts are just thoughts, they are no more real than a movie at the cinema. I know they can appear very real and feel very powerful, but next time you find yourself engaging with your thoughts, just stop and notice what's really happening. Shine the light of awareness into the darkness and you'll notice that the thought-movie in your mind is not real. And when you do that and can detach from the habit, those thoughts – and the emotions that go with them – totally lose their power.

The source of your success is yours, on the inside, and that's where you should look for your guidance. Look to your deep inner knowing and your intuition.

The things on the outside will line up just fine once you sort out the part on the inside.

STEP BY STEP DOWN THE YELLOW BRICK ROAD TO YOUR HAPPY SUCCESS

Let's work one stuck situation all the way through now that you have all of the information you need…

What Are You Stuck With?

Pick just one part of your life that you would like to make a difference in… something physical, something on the outside.

Now, for that part and that part only, just have a think about how you know that you are unhappy with it. What are the thoughts that you have? What do you tell yourself about that particular situation?

It's Really Just a Thought

If you're not sure, just think about it right now and note down the thoughts that immediately come to mind. These are just thoughts, remember, but I know it might feel a little odd. After all, I'm sure they do seem very real to you, but the truth is that the more real they feel and the more urgency they seem to have, the more you need to do this.

Just write down what you are telling yourself about the situation. What are you making up?

These silly examples might just help you along:

Thought – 'She never makes an effort any more.'
Made-up meaning – 'She must have gone off me.'

Thought – 'He never picks up his clothes.' Made-up
meaning – 'He has no respect for me.'

While not making an effort or not picking up clothes may be fact, and no doubt very disappointing or annoying, neither necessarily means anything at all.

When you give thoughts power you are then focusing on a far more serious and scary scenario that can very quickly spiral out of control: 'That's right he has no respect for me at all, I should never have married him, my was mother right, I should have known, all the signs that he was disrespectful have been there since the start if only I'd noticed, oh god I'm so stupid and now I'm stuck in a crappy marriage with no respect, what kind of person would allow that to happen? A weak one, that must be why he doesn't respect me, it's cause I'm weak, well, I'll show him who's weak, that's it, I've had enough, I'm out of here… I want a divorce!'

Now, I know it's an extreme example, but if you tell me that a train of thought spiralling out of control like that has never happened to you, I'll tell you that you're lying!

So where do you think the easiest place to make the biggest change might be?

Awareness

What's the most (or most comically) wrong you have ever been? As you know, we often make the mistake of just blindly following our thinking. What's the biggest or funniest wrong turn you've taken? Any why do you still trust it?

We give thoughts the power to hurt us when we engage with them and believe in them. Thoughts have no power of their own. And a thought with no power is a thought with no point.

Consider, instead, how different it would be if when the thought 'He never picks up his clothes' popped into your head, that would be it, nothing more. It doesn't mean anything, all it means is 'he doesn't pick up his clothes…' There could be many reasons why, but making them up is not helping!

So, for the situation you are working with just now, I'd like you to notice first of all what you are telling yourself, and then what meaning you are giving to it.

Take as much time as you need, and if you're struggling why not just close your eyes and go back to the last time it happened, and as you relive the events just note down the thoughts you were having at the time.

When you've got that you'll be ready to move on to the next stage.

All we are doing is forcing your awareness onto the outside and revealing the underlying code so that you can clearly see what's been going on all the time.

Most of the time it all happens so quickly that it's easy to miss. Once you have awakened that consciousness, though, you'll be well on the way to turning up your awareness and seeing what was previously hidden and has been shaping your life without your even being aware of it.

Can you see how the thoughts you've been having and the meaning you've been giving them have been affecting you all along? Now that we know what's going on in the background that's pulling you out of shape, it's time to figure out what to do about that.

The Map of Learning and the Compass of Knowing

For this, as you know, we have two really good tools: our map of learning and our compass of knowing.

Let me just remind you what I mean again now. The map of learning is really all the things you have learned throughout your life so far – facts, information, stuff. All the little gems and pearls of wisdom, and of course all the really big clunky bits, too. All the logical stuff, if you like. But we know that logic is not always the best way to navigate through life. We know that there is far more than can be measured by logic alone, and that if we focus just on the logical we'll be missing at least half of the picture – and it's that half, the 'illogical' half if you like, that is going to be your truest guide.

Intuition, by definition, is not logical, not something you can measure or put in your pocket or even explain. It's just a feeling, maybe just a hunch or maybe, like me, you struggle even to give it a name. It's just that thing that lets you know if you're on the right path or not.

I hope that by now you have been practising how to listen to your intuition and that you're beginning to trust it a bit more? Every time you get a hunch about something just go with it, even if it's only to find out where it takes you. If it takes you somewhere even slightly interesting, just go with it again and again until you fully learn to know and trust your inner wisdom.

With that I mind, what do you already know to do about fixing this particular situation that you're not happy with?

If nothing comes up instantly for you, just sit in a quiet place, close your eyes and take a few nice deep breaths in and out. Just allow yourself to slow down, slowing your breathing first and then your thoughts. Just allow yourself to slow all the way down and relax. Then when you feel balanced and calm, ask yourself: 'What do I know to do'? And then stay quiet and listen. It might not be clear at first but stick with it and really listen for the small voice within or your sense of knowing. It's right there and you'll be amazed at how insightful it is.

WHAT DO I ALREADY KNOW TO DO?

Now that you have a sense of what to do, it is very possible, even probable, that along with your sense of knowing came a sense of fear or apprehension? If it didn't, congratulations and just get on with it – but if, like most people, you have a sense of knowing and a sense of fear at the same time, then stick with it here. We're getting there, but just hang in with me a bit longer.

You have the knowing and the clarity as to which path you should take, and yet something stopping you: fear!

Is the fear a real concern, though, or is it, too, just a thought?

Whatever it is that comes up as a fear, ask yourself whether that fear –

A – is true?

B – might be true but is not definitely true?

C – is made up and actually comes from something
   else?

If the answer is A, just ask yourself if there is another way to achieve your goal that would make the fear no longer true? As I'm sure you're expecting, I'm going to suggest that the best source for that answer is again on the inside. Ask and trust your inner knowing: 'How else could I do it?' Even if the answer doesn't pop up straight away, just stick with it. Do you remember the story of the woman who wanted to be a doctor? Her fear was that she wouldn't be able to afford to pay her way through medical school, but as soon as she stopped worrying and telling herself that story and just opened up to finding out, a 'chance' meeting happened that opened up the possibility of exactly what she wanted… cool, eh?

If the answer is B, ask yourself what's the meaning you give to the fear that leads you to think it's true? Then notice that the meaning is probably made up and not real. The problem is that we need to make sense of things, so when a thought pops in your head your brain immediately tries to make sense of it and give it some context. It has to create a framework to house this new idea, but in reality this framework is just something you have made up to support the original thought. Just as if I randomly say the word 'button' now. Your brain will probably go off and give that some context by picturing a TV or a remote control or a control panel. It did, didn't it? But none of those things exists other than in your mind in order to give some context to the word 'button'. I was actually thinking of the one on my coat, it's a bit loose... But what you did just there was make something up to try to make sense of that one word, a best subconscious guess, if you like, but I'm sure you wouldn't want to base your life on that anymore. Would you?

Can you see how that might not be very helpful?

So, going back to you and the area you're feeling stuck with, just notice that you have spotted the hidden meaning and feel proud that you have taken a step towards setting yourself free.

If your answer was C, recognize that you have spotted one of those previously hidden thoughts that would have ruled your life, and feel proud that you've spotted it. You don't need to do anything with it, that one will almost certain have lost its power. They tend to do that as soon as you see thoughts for what they really are. Just as in the cinema if a sudden interruption breaks your suspension of disbelief and brings your awareness back to the fact that you are in a big room with lots of other people. When you notice and recognize a thought as just a thought, it loses its power.

You might, though, just like to take this opportunity to reflect on what might have happened if you had a 'B' or 'C' answer and had left them unnoticed or, worse, just accepted them as definitely being true, when in fact they *could* be just thoughts?

Who Are You Kidding?

Can you see how this is going to make a huge difference in your choices and therefore in your life? You are taking control back for yourself and breaking the habit of reacting to your thoughts.

I know it might feel a bit clunky at first, or even like hard work, but the best bit about this whole process is that it will very quickly become unconscious, you won't even notice it in time – but first you have to make it very conscious and deliberate so you can work with it and change for good.

It's the same way with learning anything new; we all go through the four stages of learning, so don't worry. Oh, and spot the 'Oh I'll never be able to keep this up' thought just now. That's just a thought, too…

Stage One – You don't know what you don't know. This is where you were when you first picked up this book. Most people are blissfully unaware of the role that 'thought' plays in their lives. Actually, that's not strictly true – if it were blissful there wouldn't be a problem. So, most people are unaware of thought and the role it plays in shaping how they feel day to day and even moment to moment. Feelings just seem to happen to them and they feel bad or make bad decisions for apparently no reason at all – well, there is a reason, 'thought', but you know that now so you're well on your way to Stage Two. In fact if you've been paying attention you will already be past Stage Two. This is the stage when you become aware of what you don't know. This can be the stage where you think,

'I really suck at this' or 'I'll never get it…' but hang in there, that's just a thought, too…

I remember when I was first learning to snowboard. I had watched loads of videos (showing my age again) of people jumping off cliffs and landing gracefully, watched them carve effortlessly down steep mountains, and even on the day of my first lesson, as I stood at the foot of the nursery slope, I wondered 'How hard can it be?' Well, the answer, as it turned out, was very! My resulting bruises to butt, knees and ego will testify to the need for much better balance and skill than I am naturally blessed with. Very quickly I had moved from Stage One to Stage Two. With the effortless assistance of gravity I had learned exactly what I didn't know, and boy did it hurt.

Having said that, I really did want to get better and be able to join my friends on the slopes, so I stuck with it. Of course I fell over many more times, but each time I got back up, picked the snow out of whichever orifice it was wedged in, and carried on. I knew I had to get past this bit before it could even start to get easier. I guess I'd just resigned myself to the fact that I was going to have to fall over lots of times before I could stand and glide, but when I did it would all have been well worth it.

I hope this is true for you now; you have to stick with this idea of noticing your thoughts and the meaning you give to them, and then breaking the habit, and of course you're going to fall over a lot at first, notice one thought and then react to it anyway, then not notice any for a while, then spot one again but this time just letting it go. But when you nail it it's just like with snowboarding or riding a bike, once you can, you can, and there's nothing you need to do to maintain that, you just need to let it be. That's Stage Four.

But wait, before all of that there is Stage Three, the stage where, with the snowboarding, I could do it but I had to concentrate really, really hard. I could get from one side of the slope to the other and I could stop and, provided there was no one else within 50 meters of me, and no bumps, and I didn't have to look any further ahead than the end of my nose, I could sometimes make a turn… but only to the right! But still, I could snowboard, albeit very badly and not for very long, but I could do it… I could do it! Now all I had to do was get better, but I knew the really tough part was behind me and it felt so good!

I'm really hoping this is where you're at now, although with a few less bruises would be good. I'm hoping that you can do it, maybe not all the time and maybe not for very long yet, but you can do it. You can spot thoughts when you have them and stop yourself from giving meaning to them, and when you do you can enjoy the freedom that immediately comes with that.

Even on the nursery slope you can notice the difference and enjoy the ride. Very soon you'll be able to head off to the black runs and even off into uncharted territory, but by then you'll not even have to think about it, it will just be the way you are, second nature.

I used to have a meticulous routine I had to go through on my snowboard, but now I just get to the top of a hill, strap it on and off I go, I don't even think about it. It's probably the same with you and driving or speaking a second language or cooking or any of the many things you'll have learned to do so brilliantly you could do them with your eyes closed, even though at first they felt hard and odd and clunky.

You're probably somewhere between Stage Three and Stage Four just now, and that's exactly where you should be. Time and practice will be the only things you need now.

But let's go back to the example we were working with, remember that? OK, cool.

Knowing what you know now, does anything really stop you doing what you know to do?

I'm guessing not, except perhaps you might feel the need for a little bit of courage and support. The best support you can have, though, is knowing that you are doing the right thing.

There is something about knowing that you are heading back to the path that's right for you that makes getting there a whole lot easier. Even if it's not plain sailing, just knowing that you are doing the right thing makes it so much easier, and of course gives you something very powerful to check in with when you need a bit of reassurance.

We all do from time to time, but when you know you're moving in the right direction it can be a lot easier than you expect.

Effortless Energy

Do you have a clear idea of your true north, your insights, your inspiring idea yet? The thing that just effortlessly energizes you? If you don't, then really this is the place to figure that out, or at least what that is 'for now'. It may well change in time, in fact it probably will, but all you need to find now is the first stop on your true path that you just can't wait to get to. You can have that, you know, you don't have to listen to the crappy thoughts anymore… but what is it that you are heading towards? What do you want to make the next bit of your life about? It's completely up to you and it can be whatever you want. As we said earlier, this is not what you think you 'should' want or what other people want for you. And maybe the thing that you want isn't even a thing. Maybe it's a feeling or a state of mind, or more happiness or well-being or a sense of creativity and achievement? What is it that you will be able to check in with to show you that as long as you have that foundation then you must be OK and on the right path?

Do you remember I spoke earlier about how we all like to have something that we can check in with that lets us know that we're OK? It could be anything, your bank balance or your career or your children or your children's careers… But it's usually something outside of you. The problem with navigating just by those things on the outside is that by very definition when you are focused on one thing you are missing everything else, and it's in that 'everything else' that you might find the easy route to what you're seeking.

Just have a quick think about what it is that you've been checking in with so far when you've needed to know that you're OK.

Now, what's it going to be from now on? I'd like you to make a conscious decision now to check in with *something else*. Make a conscious decision to check in with your own inner compass of knowing you're on the right path and the foundation of your own well-being.

Once you know where you are heading, the only thing you have to do is keep yourself in the good intuitive place where you are being true to yourself and being carried forward effortlessly by your own innate inner desire to be the happy, loving, joyful, creative and therefore successful person you've always really been if only you'd allowed yourself the freedom to notice and then just got on with it.

I know this can all sound a bit fluffy sometimes and trust me it used to sit a little awkwardly with me but I soon changed my mind when I saw this approach getting very quick and real results in the real world. It's different for sure but actually it's only different from what you've been conditioned to believe is the right way. If left to our own devices and if we stopped listening to what we were 'supposed' to do and did what we know and are moved to do, we would find ourselves in a very good place.

This is a guide for all those who 'don't know any better' – but then, that's all of us if we allow it to be... Follow what you already know to find the authentic you state of flow and trust that you're right... you are. You know better than anyone.

It has been my pleasure to be your guide on this part of your journey. Enjoy the next bit; it can be very different if you let it...

You know, inside, all you need to...

So what are you waiting for now?

Just get on with it!

ABOUT THE AUTHOR

Ali Campbell is one of the world's leading life coaches. He has built an enviable reputation as a highly sought after motivational coach, therapist, presenter and bestselling author. As a trusted advisor to celebrities, business leaders, sport stars, rock stars and even royalty, Ali is dubbed 'Mr Fix It', and is widely featured in the media – on television, radio and in print around the world.

The path to the life you want might be a lot easier than you think. You'll learn why past history is the worst possible predictor of your future, and how to navigate your own true path to whatever you want, no matter where you are starting out from. You may have heard that you have all the resources with you already, but that's not much use if you don't know how to find them and use them to achieve what you want. Ali is famed for being able to show you exactly how, and fast!

Ali's no-nonsense, irreverent style is like an arm around your shoulder and a kick up the butt, just when you need it. He gets to the point quickly and will have you laughing your way to achieving more in your life with a sense of peace and ease than you ever thought possible.

www.alicampbell.com

NOTES

NOTES

NOTES

NOTES

NOTES

NOTES

Join the
HAY HOUSE
Family

As the leading self-help, mind, body and spirit publisher in the UK, we'd like to welcome you to our community so that you can keep updated with the latest news, including new releases, exclusive offers, author events and more.

Sign up at www.hayhouse.co.uk/register

Like us on Facebook at Hay House UK

Follow us on Twitter @HayHouseUK

www.hayhouse.co.uk

Hay House Publishers
Astley House, 33 Notting Hill Gate, London W11 3JQ
020 3675 2450   info@hayhouse.co.uk